A Baptist Opinion

for Every Occasion

A Serious Examination of Baptist Behavior

Chaplain (Colonel) Jim Rennell
U.S. Army (Retired)

LARGE PRINT EDITION

MaxHoltMedia

Scripture quotations marked:
...**NASB** are taken from the New American Standard Bible, © 1960, 1962, 1963, 1968, 1971, 1972, 1973, 1975, 1977 and 1995 By, The Lockman Foundation. Used by permission. All rights reserved.

...**KJV** are taken from the Holy Bible, King James Version, Cambridge, 1769, Used by permission. All rights reserved.

...**TMB** are taken from The Message Bible, © 1993, 1194, 1995, 1996, 2000, 2001, 2002. Used by permission of NAVPRESS Publishing Group. All rights reserved.

...**New International Version**®, **NIV**®. Copyright © 1973, 1978, 1984, 2011 by Biblica, Inc.™ Used by permission of Zondervan. All rights reserved worldwide. www.zondervan.com The "NIV" and "New International Version" are trademarks registered in the

Cover Design and Publishing: Max Holt Media
303 Cascabel Pl., Mt Juliet, TN 37122
www.maxholtmedia.com

ISBN 13: 978-1-944537-34-0
Printed in the USA by Create Space – Amazon.com

Introduction

When things were not going well in my three careers as a Baptist minister, Army chaplain, and educator, before or if the situation became desperate, I would ask my family, staff, or friends for help. In desperate times it is essential to ask for help for things you can't understand or see by yourself. I think that time has come for all Baptists to take a look at themselves, make a few changes and stop the divisiveness.

Look and read the table of contents and you will see that I am trying to be upfront about why the issues facing Baptists are complex and cannot be fixed with**...more evangelism, more missions, and more money.**

To assist the reader, I have used an ellipsis and printed in a bold font all quotes from the media, internet, or my personal opinions. Selected scriptural translations may vary for three reasons. First, I have tried to use bible verses that are often used in sermons, literature or quoted by Baptists. Second, occasionally they are slightly used out of context intentionally, as they often are in Baptist discussions. Finally, I have chosen various bible translations to show how a different interpretation gives a broader or different understanding of the scripture passage.

At one time, back in the 1980's, before computers, I had filed over 22,000 3x5 cards on subjects and topics I had read or heard about. Sometimes, in order to type, cut or paste the information on small cards, dates, sources and authors were lost or omitted to fit on the card. I apologize that I am unable to always give full credit where it is due.

One of my neighboring pastors once said in a 1954 Baptist minister's meeting, I attended...**When better sermons are written, I will preach them. Until then I must cut and paste good ideas and thoughts into my own sermons.**[1] **And, I wrote that down on a card.**[2]

---

[1] Todd County, KY., Baptist Association, Ministers Meeting April 1954

[2] My personal card file...now computerized as a word document file. 2,478 pages

TABLE OF CONTENTS

15 QUESTIONS THAT SHOULD BE ANSWERED

1. Why is there a Baptist opinion for every occasion? 11

2. What is the purpose of religion? 21

3. How many Baptists are there, and which ones really matter? 37

4. Who is a sinner and what is sinful behavior? 51

5. Does Baptist religious liberty and polity discriminate? 65

6. Should modernity be, accepted, changed or rejected? 83

7. Is your hermeneutic the problem? ... 97

8. Is Baptist Christianity right for everyone? 111

9. Baptist doctrine, does it really speak for God? 133

10. Who should marry, or not marry? ... 149

11. Why Baptists can't solve the
restroom question. 163

12. Which Bible translation or whose
interpretation is correct? 177

13. Who told you this is the way it
has to be? 193

14. Can Baptists stop culture wars?....... 207

15. Yes, there is a solution to the Baptist
problem! 219

About the Author 227

Chapter 1

WHY IS THERE A BAPTIST OPINION FOR EVERY OCCASION!

This is not a book about Baptist theology, although I do mention theology when discussing some subjects. It is about how Baptists practice faith and beliefs in their day-to-day world. The two terms are orthodoxy (right belief) and orthopraxy (right practice). The religious term for these words is called *Church Polity*. Polity turns out to be what a church may or may not believe or practice at the local church level. Often, polity becomes a paradox because... *a Baptist church may believe something but may not enforce it, because enforcement causes more problems.* This is also true for its members. To complicate this further, what Baptists, in different denominations and places, believe and practice, also varies among members and churches. **So, my thesis is...*that a Baptist can believe and practice just about anything, and find a Baptist church or group to do it in.***

I believe it is historically correct to say that Baptists have had an opinion, at any moment in time, since John Smyth and Thomas Helwys founded the first Baptist congregation in Amsterdam, Holland circa 1608/09.

At last count Wikipedia lists over 345,000,000 Baptists in associations, affiliations, denominations, groups, and unions worldwide.[3] Because Baptists believe in local church autonomy and soul competency, every church exercises its Baptist beliefs a little differently. If research were correctly done, there would be very few identical Baptists or churches who agree on anything. Water baptism does not earn a church or its members the Baptist title. Nearly all Baptists have a dissenting opinion about something. **By dissenting, I mean to differ in sentiment or opinion, especially from the majority.**[4] Every congregation has someone who has a disagreement about something. Baptists are a familiar breed. Most Americans have met or know a few. They are described in

---

[3] Wikipedia,
https://en.wikipedia.org/wiki/List_of_Baptist_denominations
[4] https://www.merriam-webster.com/dictionary/dissension

many ways and names. Lee Child, in his latest book, used Baptists in comparison with bikers...**Bikers were as split as Baptists. All the same, but different.**[5] They are the ones who don't like something and are quick to tell you about it, whether you want to listen to them or not. I qualify as a Baptist because I have my own dissenting opinions. My dissent comes from what I have seen, heard, and experienced as a Baptist leader in three different Baptist denominations as minister, educator, staff member and chaplain.

Right now, Baptists are like other Christian groups, trying to find answers for the rapid cultural changes that are occurring all around them. It is my view that Baptists are providing answers, but not the ones our culture is accepting. For example, this week, two different bank employees shared with me they were both raised Baptist and now neither attends church. Baptist solutions, in the past, focused on evangelism, bigger churches and staffs with more revenue for missions. Their communities however, are not seeing churches

---

[5] The Midnight Line, Lee Child, Delacorte Press, 2017, page 11

or members practicing anything near the lifestyle they preach. Evangelism is falling on deaf ears. **New buildings, with lots of special facilities, are not reaching busy families.**[6] Churches are shifting members from one to another, but not growing. So what theology, doctrine and lifestyle changes are Baptists willing to make to be successful in a changing culture?

In towns and cities seventy-five years ago, citizens believed that church membership and attendance were a requirement. Guilt, shame and a loss of respect were the methods used to get them forgiven, saved and attending.

Today, this approach is not working. Unbelievers and non-Christians are becoming the majority. Secularism has pretty much determined what goes on television and is in the news. They have removed prayer from public schools, accepted abortion, civil rights and gay marriage. Politicians quote religious values, but vote secular when push comes to shove. It is hard for Baptists to change their ways when cultures change. So, different times

---

[6] Autopsy of a Deceased Church by Thom S. Rainer, - The Church Obsessed Over the Facilities

call for solutions that care for people rather than promoting programs, and critical judgments that drive them away.

How can a Baptist church today let its voice and work be heard and seen in a way that makes a difference? Walk with me through these chapters. Think, before making a judgment at what I suggest. Maybe start a discussion that will evaluate, adapt, or adjust my thinking. Some of my opinions may start a conversation that leads to more or better changes I have not considered. A few Baptist churches have already started making changes and are making an impact on their community, as well as adding quality to what it means for others to be a Baptist. Take a look at them and see what they are doing that is different.

Complaining about a secular, non-religious world is not changing it. A Methodist minister who writes a religious column for a local Tennessee newspaper is inundated with complaints about his theology and point of view. He collected his critics, castigations, and opinions; printing them in a book titled *Bullied in the Bible Belt*. Letters to him, and his editor, state that...**he is evil and trying to destroy**

Christianity (and) his belief in the Bible. He must not be a Christian.[7] Some of those who complained about his articles are Baptists, because I have talked to one or two who are.

Others have adopted that unique Baptist characteristic of dissenting and disagreement. What does it mean to be a dissenter if you can't give your opinion? Such thought-patterns or attitudes are not unique to Baptists in the United States. It is a cultural habit for Baptists around the world. They not only disagree with you and me, but each other, over what is best for this world by giving you their best Baptist interpretation.

Baptists love their autonomy and will never give it up. The result...*there is no one Baptist point of view on any subject.* An old, humorously told, Baptist joke tells others how our dissenting nature works...**Whenever two Baptists are in a discussion, there will always be three opinions. Each will have his or her own point of view on the topic; then a third view will be their agreement on a few minor points.**[8] Why? For a Baptist to

---

[7] Summarized quotes from the book, Bullied in the Bible Belt

[8] Author's card file -

have an opinion, shows they have some knowledge of religion, the Bible, Christianity, politics, and cultural thoughts on the world that need to be discussed. Especially, if they think there is a biblical application. Then, with knowledge and information, they have the right to disagree, on any subject.

Using a particular biblical interpretation supplies a reason to be heard, even if no opposing opinion is asked for. Doesn't the Bible say, *"Let the redeemed of the Lord say so, who he hath redeemed from the hand of the enemy.*[9] This is the Baptist premise for most social discourse. It doesn't matter if statements are negative or positive. Their point of view needs to be heard. Besides, what kind of world would this be if people always agreed on everything? Baptists claim their right to dissent.

It seems that differences about how Baptists think and behave can usually be found in any place where Baptists live. Liberal Baptists do not approve of fundamental Baptists, and vice versa. There are at least a hundred different Baptist groupings who

---

[9] Psalm 107:2 (KJV)

disagree in theology and church polity, among themselves or within the same denomination. Some Baptist churches disagree over Bible translations, hymnals, or religious literature within the same city or association.

Baptist churches have ministers and members who disagree on theology and church polity. There are foot-washing Baptists, some who speak in tongues and others who worship on Saturday. They disagree over civil rights, social justice and the proper application of the social gospel. A few Baptists disagree over wine or grape juice used for communion and who they will or will not accept as members from other denominations without re-baptism.

A few Baptists might agree and admit that they are biased on social or theological issues. So, to be fair, Baptists will agree or join with other denominations on issues, if they can be the ones to state how the issue is worded. Words are important. So, to get Baptists to join or agree on an issue, you have to agree to let them determine what the words mean. Failure to do so, could mean there will be disagreements over how the issue is proposed or discussed.

A topic might be something as simple as…*When is abortion right or wrong?* A Baptist might disagree with this wording because the correct statement should be… **abortion is always wrong.**[10] Such a topic would prolong any discussion because it is not about the *when is an abortion appropriate*, but *why the Baptist position this topic is always biblically and rightly stated.* If Baptists can agree on…*the wording, then the definition usually leads to the right conclusion… theirs.* It just doesn't pay to disagree with a Baptist when they are right in their definitions.

Of course, there are Baptists opinions and points of view that are sound, unbiased, well researched, and/or intelligently stated. This can be a positive thing because somewhere in all their differences, there are thoughts, ideas, and points of view that can be creative, thoughtful, challenging, or worthy of consideration. But, it's hard to wade through the verbiage and get to what is important about how, when or where truth applies.

10

http://www.sbc.net/resolutions/search/results.asp?query=abortion

In any discussion, Baptists can be difficult because they do not agree or speak with one voice on any topic or issue. Historians suggest that dissension increased when Luther, Zwingli, and others broke away from the Catholic church. In 1607 a small group left England for Amsterdam. Soon after arriving they started baptizing each other. Their detractors, on the continent, named them Anabaptists because, having been baptized as infants into the Church of England, they wanted to be re-baptized as adult believers. This distinction, or detraction depending on your point of view, led to the name *Anabaptist,* sticking. Baptists today kept the name but are still in disagreement with faith, culture, politics, or personal values, morals or points of view. It is in their nature to be like this.

If you finish this book, you should be able to understand why Baptists are all over the compass on any discussion or topic. It is a misinterpretation of what it means to be a Baptist if you think that, if you have seen, heard one, or even a few, you have heard them all. Baptist sub-groups are so multidimensional, it may be impossible to put their opinions into a few categories.

Chapter 2

WHAT IS THE PURPOSE OF RELIGION?

The best explanation for understanding the purpose for any given religion was given to me by **Reverend Gary Harris, a retired Michigan State prison chaplain, who, like me, provided religious support in many multicultural, multi-denominational environments.**[11] He referenced Stephen Prothero's book, **God Is Not One,**[12] saying that one of the easiest way to understand differences in religions, is to look at their stated purpose: Christianity's is, forgiveness for sin to gain salvation. **For Hinduism, it's escape continual rebirth. Islam stresses submission to Allah. The purpose for Buddhism is to escape suffering.**[13] Over the years, each of these four religions have divided, splintered, and created subgroups that

---

[11] Breakfast meeting Uncle Pete's Truck Stop - Fall 2016

[12] Stephen Prothero - God Is Not One - Harper Collins 2011,

[13] Breakfast meeting - Uncle Pete's Truck Stop Restaurant Summer - 2017

sometimes, like Baptist groups, do not get along with each other. Understanding differences is the key to understanding religious subgroups. Baptists are one example and can be classified as monotheistic, evangelical, Christian, and Protestant.

No matter how much education you have on the subject of religion, you will always be a disciple and a learner. **This is particularly true when you must work with a multi-denominational, multicultural community that includes atheists, agnostics and humanists, *et all*.**[14] As a military chaplain... I found that religious differences, even within the same religion, create immense issues for commanders, service members and their families.

In keeping our nation free, the military accepts men and women who are atheists on the left and religious fundamentalists on the right. These are the people of all faiths and no faith; working and serving together to fulfill their responsibilities and duty to their nation. As a

---

[14] http://www.esquire.com/news-politics/news/a28759/religion-and-the-military-052214/

chaplain, to be effective, you must understand the stated purposes for Catholics, Protestants, Jews, Buddhists, Muslims, plus all the minority groups including Witches, Devil Worshipers and Satanists; who all want recognition, equal time and access to government resources.

Religion is a difficult subject and requires understanding and cooperation. For example: Must a Jewish or Seventh Day Baptist, service member, be forced to work on their Sabbath...**the Lord blessed the Sabbath day and made it holy.**[15] Will a Mormon, Adventist, Independent or Regular Baptist be released from duty at certain times to go to special places for prayer...**But when you pray, go into your most private room, and, closing the door, pray to your Father, who is in secret; and your Father, who sees in secret, will reward you in the open.**[16] Will the military deny a Hindu a vegetarian diet,[17] or a Muslim food not cooked in pork fat...**forbidden to you (for food) are: dead meat, blood, the flesh of**

---

[15] Exodus 20:11 (NASB)

[16] Matthew 6:6 (TAB)

[17] https://en.wikipedia.org/wiki/Hindu

swine.[18] Can a Food Service Officer refuse to provide a Kosher meal for a Jew with meat not cooked in milk...**You shall not boil a kid in its mother's milk.**[19]

Differences do matter, and Baptists are no different on issues that are important to them. For example, some Baptists in the same congregation might believe in abortion under certain conditions, while others do not believe in it at all, and the remainder may have no opinion for or against abortion.

There may be gays who attend worship, but are not members, and are never questioned about their lifestyle. In any discussion on social issues, a Baptist congregation might have a dozen different opinions on what the government should do about gays, minorities and immigrants. Baptists are left with options: stay and fight, leave and find another church, or do not make the discussion an issue. This is not true in churches that have a hierarchical, top down structure.

---

[18] Qur'an, 5:3 - Tahrike Tarsile Qur'an, Inc.

[19] Deuteronomy 14:21 (NIV)

Baptist churches are governed, based on **…the doctrine of soul competency,**[20] which allows every individual the right to interpret scripture for themselves. Baptist scholar, E. Y. Mullins, wrote…**the principle of the competency of the soul in religion under God is a distinctive Baptist contribution to the world's thought.**[21]

So, individual differences do and should matter. Is there a way to understand Baptists' differences as they travel their religious journey from church to community? Yes, and I will share with you examples of how Christians work together in the military.

Sometimes, a service member's religious point of view can complicate the mission when there is more than one reason to overcome the enemy. Usually the first is to stop enemy aggression and bring peace. The second depends on the circumstances and situation. For some service members the battle option

---

[20] https://soundfaith.com/sermons/33501-baptist-foundations-soul-competency
[21] www.baptistdistinctives.org/resources/articles/is-soul-competency-the-baptist-distinctive

may mean destroying the aggressor's religion or culture. **For great is the LORD and most worthy of praise; he is to be feared above all gods. For all the gods of the nations are idols, but the LORD made the heavens.**[22]

It took me a minute or two to respond when two soldiers coming back from Iraq asked if it was okay, as Baptists, to hate and kill Muslims. Should I have responded... **Love your enemies, do good to those who hate you, bless those who curse you, pray for those who mistreat you. If someone slaps you on one cheek, turn to them the other also. If someone takes your coat, do not withhold your shirt from them?**[23]

Some chaplains, using the same bible I do, but representing other faith groups, may have responded differently to these Baptist soldiers...**Moses built an altar and called it The Lord is my Banner. He said, because' hands were lifted up against the throne of the Lord, the Lord will be at war against the**

---

[22] 1 Chronicles 16:25 (NIV)

[23] Luke 6:27-29 (NIV) New International Version

Amalekites from generation to generation.[24] Religious wars are fought over lesser issues than these.

Chaplains must stay within their governmental rules when assisting in public and private religious expression.[25] Service members have the right to practice their religion, but it must be within the government's purposes and guidelines. But, whose religion is right? Which rules will or will not be enforced? **Mormons, Mennonites, Amish, Adventists, or humanists, spiritualists or secularists all have different purposes for each person and faith group.**[26] Who was Jesus talking about, Jews or Christians, when he prayed...**they are in the world...keep them in thy name which thou hast given me, that they may be one.**[27] If Jesus was talking to Jews, and you want to be picky about details, then nothing he said

---

[24] Exodus 17:15-16 (NIV)

[25] The Military Chaplain, Volume 90, Number 1, Spring 2017 - Ethics and Role Conflict

[26] The Military Chaplain, Volume 90, Number 2, Summer 2017 Defining Spirituality pages 32-34

[27] John 7:11 (RSV)

applies to Christians until later when his...**disciples were called Christians first at Antioch**.[28] It is wrong for service members to use their religious convictions as a reason to kill an enemy combatant?

Baptists may be one in name, but they definitely are not Jews. Some accept part of the Old Testament, others, all or none of it. Sometimes, Baptists are more like those Paul wrote about in his letter to the Corinthians...**I hear that there be divisions among you.**[29] They may believe in the idea of oneness, but they may or may not be one in Christ with someone they disagree with. Claiming the name *Christian*, does not mean everyone agrees on theology, doctrine and polity. Killing the enemy for religious reasons is a poor decision.

I discovered, when writing a masters' thesis, that life in a Baptist church can be as precarious as it is in the military, or a prison. A hundred years ago, **Baptists in Tennessee**

---

[28] Acts 11:26 (NASB)
[29] 1 Corinthians 11:18 (KJV)

and Kentucky met monthly on Saturdays to judge and exclude members for various sins.[30] Who you were, and what sin you committed, would determine your future standing. Women were excluded for immodest dress and gossip and men, for drunkenness and profanity. How can there be a stated purpose for Baptists when they can't agree among themselves on which sinner gets to stay in the church and who is booted out?

It has always been this way according to scripture...**Some men came down from Judea and began teaching the brethren. Unless you are circumcised according to the custom of Moses, you cannot be saved.**[31] Jewish Circumcision is an Old Testament law. Paul rejected it. On this subject today, Baptists can go either way. Today, most Christian families do not consider circumcision a religious custom. Like most religions today, theology, doctrine and church polity are seldom

---

[30] James Earl Rennell, A History of Religious Education in the Six Baptist Churches in Bethel Association, Todd County, Kentucky 1965, Austin Peay State University, Clarksville, TN

[31] Acts 15:1 (RSV)

discussed, enforced or made an issue. **I do not believe this is as true with social issues or cultural changes which get more attention.**[32]

Baptists' differences complicate most religious discussion. For some, it is the call to good works...**For we are his workmanship, created in Christ Jesus for good works.**[33] But which good works are most important? Is it denominational service in an office, a local minister in a church, a missionary in a foreign country, or laity working in the secular world? Education and salaries sometimes show preferences for some careers over others...**Now about the collection for the Lord's people: Do what I told the Galatians churches to do. On the first day of every week, each one of you should set aside a sum of money in keeping with your income, saving it up, so that when I come no collections will have to be made.**[34]

---

[32] https://billmuehlenberg.com/2017/01/04/christians-culture-wars-time-engage/

[33] Ephesians 2:10 (RSV)

[34] 1 Corinthians 16:1-2 (NIV)

Baptists take up collections every week. Most budget expenses are local church expenses on themselves for mortgages, salaries, and utilities. If the world is the mission field, why is so much spent on maintaining buildings and taking care of members? Mormon young men give two years mission work. The Salvation Army focuses on the needs of others. Most Baptist collections are spent on keeping things going as they are. Evangelical Baptists focus on pointing out the need for forgiveness of sin...**I send you to open their eyes...receive forgiveness of sins and a place among those who are sanctified.**[35]

In Mark 3:28-29, Jesus says all sin can be forgiven and Baptists believe it, but some sins must require more work or a different approach. In a Baptist church where I served, a man was considered for a music director's position. In his youth he had embezzled a small amount of money from a clothing store where he worked. He made restitution and was let go. One of the deacons suggested that if he came

---

[35] Acts 26:17-18 (The Message)

before the church and publicly confessed his sin and believed that God had forgiven him, he should be hired.

When I suggested that this was a good idea and as soon as the young man confessed his sin and said he found forgiveness, then the deacons and I would all come forward and publicly confess our sins and tell how God had forgiven us. The public confession idea was quickly dropped, and the young man was hired...**And why beholdest thou the mote that is in thy brother's eye, but considerest not the beam that is in thine own eye?**[36]

Is it just our human nature to point out the other person's sin and not our own? Christians are often like politicians, believing in refusing self-incrimination....**God is faithful and reliable. If we confess our sins, he forgives them and cleanses us from everything we've done wrong.**[37] But then, it may depend on who is being discussed.

For Baptists, how they use their resources and time shows their priorities and may be the

---

[36] Matthew 7:3 (KJV)

[37] 1 John 1:9 GOD'S WORD® Translation

best indicator for how they define their purpose. Should Baptist theology, doctrine, or polity be considered first? Paul said**... preach the word, be urgent...convince, rebuke, and exhort...do the work of an evangelist, fulfill your ministry.**[38] Baptist churches take evangelism, missions, fellowship, new construction, or community issues seriously. Sometimes, ministers are like their denominational leader who said to me**... "We are trying to see which way the crowd is going on this, so we can get out in front of it."**[39]

Even when there is agreement among two or more Baptists on a subject, there's usually some controversy on how and when a truth should be applied. As a denominational worker and Christian educator, I found it hard to get Baptists to train new members to any standard for similarity, even within the same church...**I want them to be encouraged and knit together by strong ties of love. I want them**

---

[38] 1 Timothy 4:2-4 (RSV)

[39] Dr. Grady Cauthan, Southern Baptist Sunday School Board in 1978

to have complete confidence that they understand God's mysterious plan, which is Christ himself. In him lie hidden ...treasures of wisdom and knowledge. I am telling you this, so no one will deceive you with well-crafted arguments.[40]

Religion is one of the suggested topics never to discus in public gatherings. There may be some truth in this, but maybe not if there is a Baptist present. Lifestyles are fair game for investigation and judgment. So are politics, cultural morals and values.

All religions are facing questions and serious examination concerning their place in a rapid, **culturally changing, world.**[41] The Apostle Peter writes...**But resist him, (Satan) firm in your faith, knowing that the same experiences of suffering are being accomplished by your brethren who are in the world.**[42]

In the military, that means commanders issued you an order and expect you to carry it

---

[40] Colossians 2:2-4 (New Living Translation)

[41] The Tennessean - The future of Christianity is unclear 10/27/17, page 19A

[42] 1 Peter 5:9 (RSV)

out. **For Baptists, without an emotional commitment, having heard the apostle's proclamation repeated at the end of a sermon so often and not get involved they just don't pay attention.**[43] All religious purposes are fulfilled, by attendance and when the offering is taken. After the benediction, then it goes like this... *"You get the kids Ethel, and I'll meet you with the car."* All religious duty is completed until next week.

---

[43] My experiences in three Baptist Denominations and Baptist churches.

Chapter 3

HOW MANY BAPTISTS ARE THERE AND WHICH ONES REALLY MATTER?

This question really has two parts. The first part deals with numbers and the second, with its importance. Baptists' numbers world-wide, according to the Baptist World Alliance, are 345,479,082, **a number representing only members from 235 Baptist bodies in 122 countries and territories.**[44] These numbers are names on a list or register somewhere. Some church membership registers contain people's names who are deceased, and the church has not been informed of their demise or taken the time to update their membership.

There are other churches where members have moved away and joined another Baptist church or another denomination. This means that some names on the list are now non-Baptists and counted in two different denominations. Some on the list never asked

---

[44] https://www.bwanet.org/about-us2/stats

to have their names removed, even though they are no longer attending. Thousands of Baptists are counted more than once or should not be counted as a Baptist at all. Baptists have a variety of solutions for this problem. Unless there is guidance, each church is autonomous and membership numbers depend on who is counting and why they are carried on a register as important.

Numbers count, *because Baptists say that numbers count.* Larger numbers mean more church construction. Bigger buildings mean more influence and which important people will attend for lots of reasons. Years ago, I took part in a county-wide revival held in the Austin Peay State University football stadium. I was on the platform, with the guest evangelist. As we looked out on the crowd, he asked me to guess the attendance. We only used stadium bleachers on one side. It was a small stadium, so I estimated attendance at 300-400. He disagreed. He held up his hand, and said... **"You can't be right, watch! Now, the distance between my thumb and forefinger is about six inches. So, let me count the people sitting on a bleacher from the top** *down."* **His estimation, using the six-inch hand method, was 1150 to 1200.**[45]

This was a better number to report in the local paper's next edition. Such fanciful counting, took place in my Florida church. I walked past one of our usher's and asked how many were there. **He smiled held up his counter gizmo and replied...** *"How many do you want?"*[46]

Jesus prayed to the Father for his disciples saying...**and none of them is lost except but the son of perdition.**[47] Accepting Jesus's statement, most ministers will count or agree on numbers, as long as Satan isn't included. So, they do believe in numbers, even if there is little agreement on quality or quantity...**Not forsaking our own assembling together as the habit of some is, but encouraging one another: and all the more, as you see the day drawing near.**[48] It has often been said in Baptist circles that ministers' reputations and

[45] ps://en.wikipedia.org/wiki/Bill_Glass - Montgomery County Crusade, Clarksville, TN 1970

[46] South Venice Baptist Church, Venice, FL 1999

[47] John 17:12 (RSV)

[48] Hebrews 10:25 (NASB)

churches' importance are built on attendance, not changed communities.

It may be illegal if you vote more than once in a federal election, even if you own property in several states. But it is not illegal to belong to more than one Baptist church or another denomination at the same time. Some members transfer from one congregation to another with a formal letter dismissing them from the old congregation.

Baptists years ago, used to use the phrase...**Of like faith and order.**[49] Today, what counts is that the congregation is glad someone made a decision to join...**Honor all men. Love the brotherhood. Fear God. Honor the emperor.**[50] My experience with Baptist churches' attendees is that there are three kinds; those that come almost every Sunday; those few that come once or twice a quarter, or occasionally and should be numbered with the guests and visitors.

Some churches pass an attendance registry, asking members and visitors to sign-

---

[49] Churches where I was the minister or belonged

[50] 1 Peter 2:17 (RSV)

in. Others are opposed to signing-in. Such programs have good intentions but might intrude on Baptist independence or privacy by forcing attendees and visitors to register and get on a mailing list. Remember, dissent is a Baptist option. It will probably not be long before larger Baptist churches will buy facial recognition software for their televised services so there will be no escaping who attended and who didn't. Congregations can then be scanned for proof you were there.

Some churches are accepting credit cards instead of cash ...**if any of you agree on earth about anything they ask, it will be done for them by my Father in heaven. For where're two or three are gathered in my name, there am I in the midst of them.**[51] I guess checking attendance and credit card giving is going too far... or is it?

The Second part of this chapter's title deals with who is important. Baptists are big on importance because...it says who you are and what is your standing in the community, state, nation. Bigness, such as the largest Protestant

---

[51] Matthew 18:19-20 (RSV)

denomination in America, must indicate that your witness, voice or opinion on an issue must be considered.

Why else would John Kennedy seek out Baptists in Texas to explain why, as a Roman Catholic, he would not let the Pope speak for him on issues related to his presidency?[52] Texas Baptists are a large voting body; he needed their votes. Yes, there are theological differences between Texas Baptists and Catholics, but the two will work together for presidential elections, on sexual, gender or abortion issues, if they can agree on the person, wording, or issue. If all Texas Baptists agreed on a candidate, the odds are very favorable that the candidate would win.

Baptists seldom talk about membership or attendance, unless to prove something. Small classrooms may be good for students in a school or university, but in big Baptist church sanctuaries, even if they are only half filled, numbers tell the community who is important.

In one community, the Baptists remolded and added height to their steeple, so it was the

---

[52] JFK speech September 12, 1960

tallest steeple in town. Big buildings and numbers show who is important. It is unusual for Baptists to share their facilities with other congregations, unless they are a satellite of the mother church and can be counted in the numbers game.

Wanting to be recognized as a witness for Christ can be a good thing. So, Baptists focus attention toward publishing worship services times, social events and activities. For Baptists the...**most segregated time of the day is the Sunday service.**[53]

When white segregation in churches happens, it is usually at every level: race, gender, age, activity, worship style, parking, location, furniture, community leaders, and the list goes on. There is a trend among some Baptists to add worship to other days and times. Baptists in the 1940's up to 1980's had programs on Sunday night, followed by an evening worship service. Slowly, however, because of more and more competition for time, Baptists began losing power to control

---

[53] https://www.theodysseyonline.com/cultural-diversity-church

what community activities were allowed on Sundays and Wednesdays nights.

I served in a denomination that once had a program emphasis for more Sundays than there were in a calendar year.[54] Now, in some churches, politics is emphasized from the pulpit. **The Pew Research Center found that 68 percent of white evangelicals identify as Republican, while 82 percent of black Protestants identify as Democratic.**[55]

As the nation becomes more divided on social and political issues, **the carryover into churches is a reason for attendance losses.**[56] I wish I had kept track of the numbers of church members who felt that changing values, morals and social issues were sure signs for **the second coming of Jesus.**[57]**...Now we request you, brethren, with regard to the coming of our Lord Jesus**

---

[54] 1 Corinthians 9:22 NIV)

[55] https://www.nae.net/black-white-race-american-denominations/

[56] ww.pewforum.org/2008/10/23/how-church-attendance-affects-religious-voting-patterns/

[57] https://billygraham.org/decision-magazine/february-2009/proclaiming-christs-return/

Christ and our gathering together to Him...let no one deceive you.[58] Things like these were important in the past, but now, lacking numbers, they are becoming unimportant. Prayer meetings and bible studies were held on Wednesday nights with mission activities for children and youth.

There were always choices for what kind of literature was to be used in Sunday school. Most churches used their own denominational literature. Others chose more conservative, non-denominational evangelical publications. Now, even that is changing...**Study to show thyself approved unto God, a workman that needed not to be ashamed, rightly dividing the word of truth,**[59] is losing steam. Baptists in the past did most of this within their denominational printing houses.

Now however, there is so much disagreement over emphasis on gender, race and content, that congregations are choosing literature that agrees with local church doctrines and polity. Evangelism and

---

[58] 2 Thessalonians 21-2 (NASB)

[59] 2 Timothy 2:15 (KJV)

attendance promotions seem to be the major reasons. In my opinion, when education takes a back seat to evangelism, future Baptists will become more self-centered, focusing only on themselves and believing what the minister tells them, is truth.

Who the Baptists are and what they think they are does matter. Scripture warns them that they…**should not to think more highly of himself than they ought.**[60] So without naming names, I can provide some of the characteristics that do seem to matter. Churches and ministers are both guilty of thinking that bigger is better. Baptists are fond of new bigger buildings with the hope of drawing larger numbers; interestingly at a time of dwindling memberships.

In a world that is filled with problems and issues needing care from God's people, is there really a need for more million-dollar mega churches, built on huge campuses in communities surrounded by poverty and citizens out of work? **The development of a megachurch culture has, however,**

---

[60] Romans 12:7 (NASB)

produced a significant backlash, with critics often railing against theological superficiality, vapid worship music, and a seeker-sensitive, consumeristic ethos.[61]

Is it really important for a Baptist church to have a bowling alley, basketball courts, and parlors with decorator furniture? As the nation divides more and more between the haves and have nots, where is the church in its ministries to the homeless, the poor, single parent, and working parents? One of my Baptist Seminary friends showed me his diamond stick pin at a convention, saying it was a gift from his rich church, who wanted him to look like his members.

Baptists think televising services is important. Yes, they do bring ministry to those who are shut-in or can't attend, but it is expensive and can be for the wrong purposes if the church wants to prove they are the top church with this televised ministry. I suppose such extravagance is to be accepted since

---

61

http://www.christianitytoday.com/ct/topics/m/megachurches/

Jesus said…**You will have the poor with you for the rest of your lives.**[62] Bigger doesn't necessarily mean better or an understanding for ministering to communities with real needs. If missions are important, why are Baptists focusing on new buildings they can't afford and now can't pay off?

In my view, we cannot solve America's problems with Christianity and only one religious view point. If Christians enjoy a tax deduction from the Internal Revenue Service, then communities should see some benefit from it, besides big buildings, diamond stick-pins, and large salaries for ministers and denominational leader's.

It's time to heed the words of our Lord…**Then the King will say to those on his right, 'Come, you who are blessed by my Father, inherit the kingdom prepared for you from the foundation of the world. For I was hungry, and you gave me food, I was thirsty and you gave me drink, I was a stranger and you welcomed me, I was naked and you clothed me, I was sick and**

---

[62] Mark 14:7 (The Message)

you visited me, I was in prison and you came to me. Then the righteous will answer him, saying, 'Lord, when did we see you hungry and feed you, or thirsty and give you drink? And when did we see you a stranger and welcome you, or naked and clothe you? And when did we see you sick or in prison and visit you?' And the King will answer them, 'Truly, I say to you, as you did it to one of the least of these my brothers, you did it to me.[63]

All of this does say something about Baptist priorities and purpose. Maybe it is time to reconsider what is important, besides numbers. If you really care about people and helping them to find healthy moral lifestyles, why count numbers at all? What is wrong about a church that cares for all kinds of people. When Baptists show they care and practice what they preach, making it a positive difference in their own lifestyle, this may influence others to think and compare lifestyles. Do they have to be like us, a

---

[63] Matthew 25:34-40 - (ESV) English Standard Version

particular kind of Baptist, or is it really a Christ-like lifestyle that counts?

Chapter 4

WHO IS A SINNER AND WHAT IS SINFUL BEHAVIOR?

It doesn't sound right to say that Baptists are big on sin, but they are. How else could they interpret this strong biblical warning...**abstain from all appearance of evil?**[64] Seminary trained Baptist ministers, learned that one interpretation for sin came from the Hebrew word that meant, *to miss the mark.* The standard then, for a Christian, was to be perfectly in the center of God's will; understanding that, anything outside of that, missed the mark.

Israel was forewarned by Moses about obedience to the Lord before entering the promised land with these words...**But if you will not do so, behold you have sinned against the Lord, and be sure your sin will find you out.**[65] It could be that Baptists are claiming that Moses' warning in this Old

---

[64] 1 Thessalonians 5:22 (KJV)

[65] Numbers 32:23 (RSV)

Testament verse, links sinful behavior with the Apostle Paul's view in his letter to the Romans...**For all have sinned and come short of the glory of God.**[66]

My Catholic chaplain friends, agreed with me that guilt was a great way to get the attention of the sinner and call for a change in behavior. For some, this warning wasn't enough; God found out and so did their First Sergeant and the Commander. Commanders care, but most people in communities today are too busy to care about the deviant lifestyles of sinners, as long as it doesn't bother them.

I used this *missing the mark* metaphor in sermons occasionally. The problem was, my congregations didn't always agree with me about *where on the missed mark* was sinful. As an inexperienced, non-seminary minister, I needed help in my first church. I asked one of my men how I was doing in my preaching. He suggested, I come down harder pointing out sin, and right over wrong. **So, I preached a sermon on the evils of tobacco.**[67] On the

---

[66] Romans 3:23 (KJV)

[67] 1 Corinthians 6:19 (RSV)

way out the door, he shook my hand suggesting I had better be careful, since as a farmer, tobacco was his main cash crop and a source for my salary. I should preach on somebody else's sin, and not my farmer's for growing tobacco. I asked for his opinion, he gave it and I got it.

In another discussion on what young people should not do inside a Baptist church, one faithful church lady stood, stated that "*sin is sin*," and sat down. I think what she was referring to was the soft drinks I was serving to the youth at Sunday night activities, before the evening service. Soft drinks for her, were definitely *missing the mark*. One of her supporters agreed saying...**Soft drinks were never served in this church when I was young.**[68] My immediate interpretation for her statement was, back in her days everything her momma said about youthful behaviors was sinful.

One of the Baptists' oddest ways to describe the sin/sinner issue is, *...When someone describes that what you were doing*

---

[68] Oolitic Baptist Church, 1968

is sinful, then you are a sinner because you did it…and they said so. The bible teaches…**For while you were in the flesh, the sinful passions, which were aroused by the Law, were at work in the members of our body to bear fruit for death.**[69] Sin is sin and Baptists believe it couldn't be any clearer than that.

This all sounds so easy, but getting the right application is more difficult. Baptists are told they are not to judge others, but they can judge the fruit on the tree…**So then, you will know them by their fruits.**[70] There you have it. A youth with a soft drink in church before a Sunday night worship service is on the way to lawlessness and rebellion against parents.

In the late 50s, I brought Billy Graham and Moody Bible Science Institute films to show to young people on Sunday night fellowships before or after church. Young people came and brought their friends. Attendance grew weekly. Sunday night worship attendance also increased. Then, rumors started and squashed the actives because the 1950s movies were

---

[69] Romans 7:5 (NASV)

[70] Matthew 7:20 (NASV)

still considered sinful...**For all that is in the world, the lust of the flesh and the lust of the eye and the pride of life is not of the Father, is of the world.**[71] Billy Graham was fine, but his movies just couldn't make a passing grade. Movies, like soft drinks, were sinful.

About forty years ago whether it was a sin or not, depended on who said it was or what sins were bad in that church or community. In one Kentucky community, smoking was a sin as preached in most Baptist churches in the area. But one small rural Baptist church pastor, I knew, smoked cigars with his men before services started. Oh, but of course, no smoking was allowed inside the church, so they smoked outside...**exhort one another daily, while it is called today; lest any of you be hardened through the deceitfulness of sin.**[72]

I knew a minister of a large city church who took church tour groups to Israel. He was listed as a bi-vocational minister by his denomination

---

[71] 1 John 2:16 (RSV)

[72] Hebrews 3:13 (KJV)

because he made more money as a tour guide than he did as minister of a large Baptist church…**For the love of money is the root of all evil: which while some coveted after, they have erred from the faith, and pierced themselves through with many sorrows.**[73]

Smoking may or may not be sinful. But, taking tour groups for money to Israel did not count as sin. Okay! My mistake. Baptist, ministers and congregations are not without choices. In a world supposedly filed with sin and sinners one doesn't have to be an expert to point out people who are different. My question is…*what value is there in identifying sinners, if this is the only purpose?*

Early Christians saw themselves as change agents and wanted to have an impact on the world. **They shared their bread with each other and the members of their community.**[74] They saw the change and sought out the believers for the good news. It is different today. When the world sees self-righteousness with no attempt to change

---

[73] 1 Timothy 6:10 (KJV)

[74] Acts 2;46-47 (NASB)

themselves, there is little motivation to join with the critics and naysayers.

The conservative Christian message today is *forgiveness for sin to gain eternal life.* Heaven is the goal. While we live in this world, what really is important is getting a good place in heaven. For hundreds of years, Christians, understood how the road was to be travelled. Now, in the 21st century, sin is starting to be redefined. Take Paul's letter to the Corinthians stating…**Know ye not that the unrighteous shall not inherit the kingdom of God? Be not deceived: neither fornicators, nor idolaters, nor adulterers, nor effeminate, nor abusers of themselves with mankind, or thieves, nor covetous, nor drunkards, nor revilers, nor extortioners, shall inherit the kingdom of God.**[75]

Unless public laws are broken, there are no convictions today for coveting, drinking, reviling, idolatry, adultery, and homosexual behavior. Unbelievers and Christians, who no longer attend, today just don't care what Baptists consider sinful. Door-to-door

---

[75] 1 Corinthians 6:9-10 (KJV)

evangelism, county wide crusades, and the old two-week revival meetings are almost forgotten. It wasn't the sinner or a liberal care-free Christian who made the decision to stop having them. Baptist ministers can't get enough interest from members to take the time and effort to reach out to the lost and unsaved with more meetings. Baptists, now days, vote with their feet. As terrible as it may sound, most Christians today are not interested in convicting sinners.

I have been taught and believe that once God has forgiven sin, it was forgotten and taken away forever. God no longer counted it against you...**As far as the east is from the west, so far has He removed our transgressions from us.**[76] Like the criminal who has done the time, the judgment is completed, finished, over. But, Baptists sometimes just can't or won't go quite that far. You see, it all depends on who is the sinner and what is the sin. Then, sin may not be forgiven as far as from the east to west.

---

[76] Psalm 103:12 (RSV)

A woman joined the Army Reserves and was assigned to the unit where I was the chaplain. I discovered she was looking for a church and wanted to sing solos for worship. I invited her to our church and she joined our worship.

In time, the music director welcomed her into the choir and she began singing solos for worship. She told me she was divorced, had a troubled past, and felt God had forgiven her. Now, she was trying to start a new life. But, it wasn't long before her past caught up with her...**For while we were in the flesh, the sinful passions, which were aroused by the Law, were at work in the members of our body to bear fruit for death.**[77]

Three church members soon found out. They came to me to share their gossip. The bottom line for these women was, she might be forgiven, she could be a member of our church, but she shouldn't sing. **For judgment will be merciless to one who has shown no mercy; mercy triumphs over judgment**[78] Why? Was

---

[77]Romans 7:5 (NASB)

[78] James 2:13 (NASB)

it because she was pretty, attended services regularly, had a beautiful voice, praised God with her solos, or wanted to live a Christian life? No, she was divorced and had a troubled reputation. What would the community think if she sang in our worship services? Fortunately, she soon married a fine Christian man, left our church and lived happily ever after in another community.

We may repent, and the good Lord may forgive us our sin and Baptists will forgive but, there are those who never forget. And, the distance between the East and West isn't a part of the discussion...**Progress is impossible without change, and those who cannot change their minds cannot change anything.**[79]

In my opinion, any attempt that tries to identify sin in any person for any reason without an effort to assist them in finding a better way, is in itself a sinful activity. George Bernard Shaw once said...**the worst sin toward our fellow creatures, is not to hate them, but to**

---

[79] Romans 2:1-3 (ESV)

be indifferent to them: that's the essence of inhumanity.[80]

Identifying sinful activities is really easy. Assisting those whose habits and lifestyles that need improving is more difficult. My view of ministry is in Jesus' words to the Apostle Peter...**So when they had eaten their breakfast, Jesus said to Simon Peter, Simon, son of Jonah, do you love me more than these? He said to him, Yes, Lord; you know that I have affection for you. He said to him, feed my lambs.**[81]

The church's ministry should always be building communities by growing better churches and people. When I found forgiveness, it gave me hope for another chance for a better life. Every Christian should be encouraged to share that discovery with others who need the same help and hope. My best interpretation of Jesus' words to Peter is, if the Lord's sheep are fed right, they learn to take good care of themselves and then they,

---

80

https://www.brainyquote.com/authors/george_bernard_shaw

[81] John 21:15 (WEB) The World English Bible

like the apostles, can help others learn how to better feed themselves. We all need a little help on the road of life. The Salvation Army has proven that their ministry is successfully bringing hope and forgiveness to society's rejects...**And as you wish that others would do to you, do so to them.**[82] A few Baptist churches have also found this ministry works.

I chose this title... *"Who is a sinner and what is sinful behavior,"* for three reasons. First, Baptists cannot agree on what is a sin. Second, they have trouble identifying who is or is not a sinner. Third, what makes this worse, in my view, is when they know or decide on the sin and the sinner, they only criticize the sin and do little to help the sinner.

Remember, it is sin to know what you ought to do and then not do it.[83] Maybe the title should have been worded...*How does not helping sinners makes me a sinner?* How much time does it take to help the sinner see a new or another option? A welcoming hand, a pat on the back, and a smile encourages all of

---

[82] Luke 6:31 (ESV) English Standard Version
[83] James 4:17 (NLT) New Living Translation

us when we are trying to get it right. If Baptists can take the time to say what they don't like, why not add a little time to offer hope and ministry to the sinner and fix the problem? I never have met the person who solved and fixed all their problems by themselves. There is something hypocritical about wanting everyone to join them in heaven, when there isn't time to help them here on Earth...**Yes, a man will say, "You have faith, and I have works." Show me your faith without works, and I by my works will show you my faith.**[84]

---

[84] James 2:18 (NASB)

Chapter 5

DOES BAPTIST RELIGIOUS LIBERTY, DOCTRINE AND POLITY DISCRIMINATE?

L et me begin by asking the reader to look at the history of Baptists in general. Baptists do not want, nor have they supported, a theocratic government ruled by a particular religion. Nor, have they wanted an official state church. They are, however, for a government that bases its laws on Christian teachings, if they can determine and agree on the teachings.

These ideas come from separatist groups who fled England because they were in disagreement with the Church of England's infant baptism policy. Taking their stand against the crown's religion would have led to confiscation of property and personal rights. As separatists, they refused and fled to Amsterdam where religious freedoms were more tolerant. **As adults, baptized again,**

they earned the name Anabaptists.[85]
**Dissent became a foundation for those who
did not believe in infant baptism.**[86] **That
dissent carried over into government
legislation in the early American colonies.**[87]
It was a *leave-us-alone* attitude.

Back then, Protestantism was a rejection of
religion from the top down.....**Anabaptists
considered the state churches beyond
reformation.**[88] The idea of just *leave-us-alone*
stood the test of time for centuries, resulting in
a new idea called *religious liberty* or *local
freedom*. It was written into the U.S.
Constitution and Bill of Rights. Now, not
satisfied with being left alone, churches are
switching back, deciding they want to get
involved in politics to determine the cultural
morals and values. Protestantism gave new
meaning to individualism, when governments

---

[85] https://en.wikipedia.org/wiki/Anabaptism

[86] Word of God Across the Ages, by Bill J. Leonard, Smyth
& Helwys Press

[87] /www.facinghistory.org/nobigotry/religion-colonial-
america-trends-regulations-and-beliefs

[88] https://en.wikipedia.org/wiki/Anabaptism, also Word of
God Across the Ages by Bill Leonard

no longer had the power to punish unbelievers for religious differences...**Depending upon how one defines individualism, the values proposed by it could either run counter to one's Christian faith or create a stronger...community.**[89]

Baptists pushed for religious liberty and got it into the Constitution. As a result, they lost the power of the state to enforce a particular religious interpretation for community morals and values. **Twentieth century theological liberalism questioned long-held doctrinal and biblical interpretations that limited cultural change and restricted certain groups and individuals to limited roles in a society.**[90] A Vanderbilt constitutional professor, talking about inequality in the Constitution wrote an article subtitled...**Inequality is not just a moral or economic problem—it threatens the U.S. Constitution itself.**[91]

---

[89] http://classroom.synonym.com/religious-individualism-in-christianity

[90] https://en.wikipedia.org/wiki/Biblical_literalism

[91] <u>Vanderbilt Magazine</u> - Summer 2017, Volume 98. No. 3, page 39

Religious liberty and local church polity provide Baptists with special opportunities, which in some instances have led to discrimination. **...Therefore, I exhort the elders among you... shepherd the flock of God among you, exercising oversight not under compulsion, but voluntarily, according to the will of God; and not for sordid gain, but with eagerness; nor yet as lording it over those allotted to your charge, but proving to be examples to the flock.**[92]

It is very important to understand the difference between Church doctrine and church polity. With a few exceptions, Baptist doctrine is determined by a group of churches. But in most churches...**polity has been described as Congregationalism with the biblical leadership of a pastor and deacons.**[93] At a local church level, members decide what doctrines become polity and guide their particular church. **But there can be a fly**

---

[92] 1 Peter 5:1-4 (ESV)

[93] http://www.Baptists.net/history/2011/08/what-are-the-main-types-of-Baptist-church-polity/

in the ointment.[94] It isn't what polity *says*, it is what polity *enforces* that counts.

Sometimes, enforcement is just gossip and rumors that push members or attendees out of a congregation. A pastor friend of mine told me about one of his church members whose daughter dropped out of school for a semester to go and help her aunt in another community. The real reason was her teenage pregnancy. Her father was a church and community leader, so nothing was done to her boyfriend, beyond gossip. In the fall, she returned to her school for her senior year.

Separation of church and state applies to any discussion where religious liberty is applicable. Here are a couple of idiomatic sayings to think about. The first says…you cannot have your cake and eat it too. The second is a little different…**you can't have it both ways.** Baptists want a State and Federal tax deduction for their contributions and giving. **They want to be excluded from local taxation for street lights, fire, and police**

94…https://www.collinsdictionary.com/us/dictionary/english/a-fly-in-the-ointment

protection when used by the church.[95] Still, wanting their independence, some churches want the right to support political candidates, but will not provide a list of names or amounts of financial contributions given through their church to candidates.

Baptists have been heavily involved in public issues like abortion, women's health care, race relations, property sales and zoning, and marriage gender laws. The latest issue is transgender use of school toilets. It is not unusual for Baptists to have rules for themselves that, sooner or later, they would like applied to a local culture or passed as state and federal law. Baptists will promote scripture verses to support views and opinions for social discourse and public behavior. But then, they do not want the government to tell them they can't discriminate. When Baptists enter into the public domain, they bring their doctrines, rules and opinions with them.

Religious liberty and *discrimination*, can be synonymous, depending on how they are used in the context. The Westboro Baptist Church

---

[95] https://churchesandtaxes.procon.org/

chooses to use its religious liberty to protest at military funerals because the Federal governments recognizes LGBT as a minority...**It is easy to see a smudge on your neighbor's face and be oblivious to the ugly sneer on your own...It's this I-know-better-than-you mentality again, playing a holier-than-thou part instead of just living your own part.**[96] **This group believes God's wrath is poured out upon military service members for the governments mistake.**[97] **Jerry Falwell's** ***homosexuals view*** **didn't go quite that far.**[98] In my opinion, posting the Ten Commandments in a public building goes beyond religious liberty. This act pushes religion on citizens who do not believe in religion or any of the Baptists' scriptures quoted to justify their display.

It is almost humorous to say it, but Baptists will go to almost any extreme for the right to express their religious liberty. Expressions of

---

[96] Luke 6:37-42 (The Message Bible)

[97] https://en.wikipedia.org/wiki/Westboro_Baptist_Church

[98]

http://abcnews.go.com/Politics/story?id=121322&page=1

religious liberty, in its many forms, allows Baptists to become separatist, discriminating, and exclusive...**For you are free, yet you are God's slaves, so don't use your freedom as an excuse to do evil.**[99] For these reasons, Baptists are identified with names like Separatist, Particular, Evangelical, Independent, Three Seed in the Spirit, Free Will Baptists or Fundamental.

Religious liberty should help to determine church polity, theology, and doctrine. But, it also shows how churches can discriminate against those they do not agree with...**If you were of the world, the world would love its own; but because you are not of the world, but I chose you out of the world, therefore the world hates you.**[100] So, if someone hates you, does that mean you are doing something right? And if no one hates you, in Jerry Falwell's view, you may be in the wrong church. Racial prejudice and misogamy against women is still prevalent in how Baptists are governed.

---

[99] 1 Peter 2:16 (New Living Translation)
[100] John 15:19 (RSV)

Jimmy Carter took his dissent and left Southern Baptists for their stand against women.[101] Baptists agree with the Declaration of Independence that all are created equal, if you let them define equality, time and place.

The Old Testament law established a theocratic government with a method for removing dissenters. Baptists do not want a theocracy, so, as dissenters, they can have opinions about public policy or laws. However, Church rights and independence must stop at the church front door and should not be used to determine who can buy or sell their products and services in a community. In a theocracy the state-church can determine morality and values. Christians are failing to realize that they can't have it both ways.

In the Old Testament, times were different. Back then, women were considered the property of their fathers and husbands. Fathers would determine who their daughters married and what money or property was exchanged

---

101

http://www.adherents.com/largecom/baptist_SBC_Carter.html

for the marriage...**If a man sells his daughter as a female slave, she is not to go free as the male slaves do.**[102] A woman's virginity was a legal and important commodity. This affected the price fathers received if a woman lost her virginity...**If a man happens to meet a virgin who is not pledged to be married and rapes her and they are discovered, he shall pay her father fifty shekels of silver. He must marry the young woman, for he has violated her. He can never divorce her as long as he lives.** [103] Some interpretations of these verses can be found today in public laws concerning rape, marriage and divorce.

For years, women were blamed if a man raped her because she did put didn't put up a fight. No bruises or marks meant consent. It took centuries for a woman's statement to equal a man's in courts. In Baptist churches, up into the 1950's and 60's, women were told they couldn't wear pants, pant-suits, or men's clothing in church...**A woman is not to wear**

---

[102] Exodus 21:7 (NASB)
[103] Deuteronomy 22:28-29 (NIV)

male clothing, and a man is not to put on a woman's garment, for everyone who does these things is detestable to the LORD your God.[104] I don't know when God changed His mind about women wearing men's clothing, but it is acceptable now for them to do so. But homosexual men wearing women's clothing is still wrong inside or outside of a church.

There are disagreements among Baptists as to which genders can hold leadership positions and what the requirements are for offices. Titles may be related to education and training or culture and geographical location, but more often it relates to male/female genders. Support varies among Baptist groups whether to ordain women as deacons. Requirements concerning gender may also differ in other church positions. Paul's letter to Timothy lists the requirements that more churches are reinterpreting so women can serve as ministers or deacons...**A bishop then must be blameless, <u>the husband one wife,</u>**

---

[104] Deuteronomy 22:5 (HCSB)

vigilant, sober of good behavior, given to hospitality, apt to teach.[105]

There are two kinds of Baptist polity. The first is what happens inside of the church. And then, it depends on who takes the lead, or has the power, numbers, and money to determine what is allowed. The other kind of polity is what influence, pressure, or control Baptists can have in their community, state or nation. Some churches or leaders take part in all these arenas. I know a man who, after serving as a Baptist minister, was divorced and left the position, then came back as a Minister of Education, and years later returned as a pastor for another Baptist church. So, church polity means, it can be wrong for one Baptist church; right for another.

A few issues effect relationships inside and outside the church. An example is the sale and use of beverage alcohol. Years ago, Baptists printed on a large poster a covenant that hung on the front wall in some sanctuaries. The covenant served as a guide for believers and a

---

[105] 1 Timothy 3:2 (KJV)

reminder that...**Wine is a mocker and beer a brawler; whoever is led astray by them is not wise.**[106] Today, that covenant is seldom seen or mentioned. Longstanding, men and women raised under the covenant have not forgotten what it said about sinfulness. Baptist polity included the words from the covenant, stating that the use of alcohol as a beverage was prohibited.

In the 1850s,[107] ministers were paid in barrels of whiskey. Not so today. Because they could not drink alcohol, then Catholics, Protestants, or unbelievers living in the same city, shouldn't even buy it. In some cities or counties where there are not enough Baptists to shut down the sale of alcohol or when laws changed, allowing purchase in a grocery store...**One Baptist pastor's wife and family, I knew, could not buy groceries in stores or eat in any restaurant that sold alcohol.**[108]

Some sins in the past, you see, were forbidden, but now when times have changed, Baptists feel it is alright now...**Don't pick on**

---

[106] Proverbs 20:1 (NIV)
[107] Author's Master's Thesis, Austin Peay State University
[108] Author's ministry in Bedford, IN

people, jump on their failures, criticize their faults...unless of course, you want the same treatment. Don't condemn those who are down; that hardness can boomerang.[109]

When Baptists disagree with each other on an issue, it is often about whose polity should be practiced. Because Baptists are called the *people of the book*; scriptures are quoted to point out the error for another church or minister's leadership. A favorite verse is...**Beware of false prophets, which come to you in sheep's clothing, but inwardly they are ravening wolves.**[110] It has been so, since the beginning of Christianity. Look at the early church fathers' writings for examples of fault-finding those with whom they disagreed. Just a casual reading of the book of Acts and Paul's letters to the churches, tells us there were polity disagreements was over the circumcision issue. Another problem was the Lord's Supper and selection of deacons for services...**a complaint arose on the part of**

---

[109] Luke 6:37-38 (The Message Bible)
[110] Matthew 7:15 (NASV)

the Hellenistic Jews against the native Hebrews because their widows were being overlooked in the daily serving of food.[111]

All of this impacts on religious liberty and the right of a local church to do their own thing. For example, churches in a particular area may join and work together on projects but disagree on who can participate. Baptists working in a particular community will refuse to participate, if participating churches ordain women, support gay rights, or gay marriage. **The Saint Patrick's Day Parade in New York City is an example.**[112] Jesus said...**Let both grow together until the harvest: and in the time of harvest I will say to the reapers, gather ye together first the tares, and bind them in bundles to burn them: but gather the wheat into my barn.**[113] Now, Christians know when to do their judging and separating.

The religious right, including some Baptist churches and hypocritical groups, shouts persecution by the media, all the while

---

[111] Acts 6:1-7) (NASB)

[112] https://www.advocate.com/politics/2017/3/10/st-patricks-day-parade-banned-gay-vets

[113] Matthew 13:30 (The Geneva Bible)

practicing discrimination....**But this does not mean that the Convention does not have a responsibility to act on its own authority. In 1992 the SBC voted to withdraw fellowship from Pullen Memorial Baptist Church in Raleigh, North Carolina and Binkley Memorial Baptist Church in neighboring Chapel Hill. Both churches had taken actions that endorsed homosexuality.**[114]

The Civil Rights legislation in 1964 put Baptists right in the center of the movement, and then later, some leaned toward a more rightist position for gender or minority issues...**2013 is likely to be remembered as the final collapse of the old, confrontational Religious Right in favor of a less partisan, more pragmatic approach.**[115] Baptists are well represented in congress, state legislatures and local elections, to include the Baptist point of view. However, the push to put God back in the schools, keep God in the National Anthem, posting the Ten Commandments in the local

---

[114] http://www.albertmohler.com/2014/06/19/Baptist-polity-and-the-integrity-of-the-southern-Baptist-convention/

[115] https://www.theatlantic.com/politics//the-changing-face-of-christian-politics

courthouse, is waning. **I find it interesting and a little hypocritical for Baptists to want their definition of God included for governmental issues and not Jews, Muslims, Mormons, Jehovah Witnesses.**[116]

When I mentioned this issue in a group, a participant responded that some of those I named, were foreign religions or cults and should not be included in the discussion. The best politicians, and citizens may not always be Baptist or deeply religious. **In the last twenty years, however, politicians are starting to relook at religious fundamentalism for its restrictive values.**[117] The minister is no longer the only one who could speak about morals, values, and what is culturally acceptable.

Nobody's perfect, and this includes Baptists.[118] In my view, it is fine to carry the name Baptist, as long as it is not a requirement for every citizen to wear it. When it is used to

[116] https://gov/blog/2016/07/22/combating-religious-discrimination-today

[117] Ray Waddle, The Tennessean, 10/7/2017 page 15a Looking toward the future of Protestantism

[118] https://www.dallasnews.com/opinion/commentary/2017/05/01/tell-difference-religious-persecution-selfishness

intentionally discriminate, I draw the line. We live in communities with all kinds of diversity. Demanding that one religious view should take precedence over another, just doesn't fit in today's world. Religious discrimination is alive and well, practicing in more places than one might want to believe in this modern era.

Chapter 6

SHOULD MODERNITY BE ACCEPTED, CHANGED OR REJECTED?

There is a popular old saying…**Nothing is permanent except change.**[119] However, with this truism, I believe some religious groups do not want to be included in the discussion. *When theology, doctrine, or polity are the determining reasons for the faith, change may be difficult.* My sixty years in ministry has proven that change can be fast or slow, and sometimes painful. In my first church, it took over three months to replace a toilet that froze and burst and two months to replace a mower to cut the grass.

Wasps were always available in the sanctuary during the summer. No effort was made to remove them. Rain, over the years, washed away the ground under the church front steps. They dropped about 4-5 inches. Older members had trouble raising their feet

---

119

https://www.brainyquote.com/quotes/quotes/h/heraclitus16 5537.html high enough to get in the door. The general consensus said, the sinking started about four or five years ago. Other ministers' stories, over the years, have confirmed that my church was not unique or unusual in this regard.

The standard answer for most Baptist churches, in any discussion when change is proposed, is...**We've never done it that way before.**[120] It has taken over thirty years for some churches to accept the changes young adults wanted for the music in worship. The results are, there are three kinds of music used in worship...**The first, were changes young adults made for more modern rhythms and words. Second, middle aged adults did accept a blending of old hymns with the new music. And finally, those seniors who said the new music would never be allowed in their church until after they were dead.**[121]

A favorite bible verse used to get members to come along for a particular point of view

---

120

http://www.ucc.org/daily_devotional_the_seven_last_words_of_the_church

[121] Author's ministry in IN, TN, KY, and FL

is...**And we know that all things work together for good to them that love God, to them who are the called according to his purpose.**[122] The question then is, who is doing the calling? Is it the old members who pay the bills or the younger adults who live in a different generation and will be the future of the church? Evolution means change and it is happening in all phases of life, including Christianity and Baptists who do not want a part in this discussion. Change sometimes happens even without aggravation or a direct intention. **Syncretism sounds like an ugly word, but it happens as values, morals, traditions and customs blend resulting in change that occurs when the old new blend to make something new or better.**[123]

Whether things are done intentionally or not, the results seem to be leading toward a decline in cooperation and attendance among Baptists. My own evaluation is that it is the old

---

[122] Romans 8:28 (KJV)

[123] https://www.tomorrowsworld.org/commentary/is-religious-syncretism-a-good-thing

idea…**just leave-us-alone attitude**.[124] Many young to middle-age adults have fled to larger churches where they can use newer and more modern facilities, have more options for programs, while hiding from responsibilities with issues they are not interested in. Larger church staffs provide money and leadership for programs that poorer and smaller churches must provide for themselves. A second reason is, older or rural churches may fear modernity. Most Baptists under forty, welcome change, if it fits with their lifestyle. Older Baptists find comfort in remaining traditional. Why is there a need to continually change? **First and foremost, is the idea some millennials have, that religious people are hypocritical, judgmental and insincere.**[125] The senior's view is, *"If the issue worked in yesterday's world, why can't it can work in todays?"* **It is a fact that different generations approach**

---

[124] https://www.9marks.org/article/journalchurch-and-churches-independence/

[125] https://www.theblaze.com/stories/2013/10/30/5-possible-reasons-young-americans-are-leaving-church-and-christianity-behind/

problem-solving with different values, morals, and choices.[126]

There is some discussion today about churches dropping the word Baptist from their name. The most common reason...**To create a clear or new priority.**[127] Currently, this movement focuses on using names like...Cornerstone, Fellowship Church, Living Way Church, The Rock, Covenant Church, et all.[128] Sometimes, polity issues end up in selecting the new name for some Baptist sub-groups. **There is an 'I Am Baptist Church', lots of 'Calvary Baptist' churches with crosses but, only one 'Little Hope Baptist' that I know of.**[129] A few names come from issues that are older than the present membership. This causes the congregation to be unaware of what elevated the issue to become a naming-problem. I know of two First Baptist churches in the same town. One is

---

[126] https://cmao-ok.org/DocumentCenter/View/204

[127] http://thomrainer.com/2014/12/six-reasons-churches-change-names/

[128] https://www.thedailybeast.com/southern-baptists-take-baby-steps-away-from-the-culture-wars

[129] Montgomery county, Clarksville, TN

African American and the other Caucasian. They used to be one church with slaves in the balcony and whites on the sanctuary floor. Now they are separate congregations in two buildings.

Today one of the most noticeable changes is that you don't have to dress up to go to church. Jeans, shorts, overalls, flip-flops or whatever is comfortable, fit in with worship. If you are looking for a different opinion that shows why Baptists have different points of view on almost any subject, look on the internet for an article titled**...7 Biblical Principles for how to dress as a Christian woman.**[130] I hope someday, someone writes an article on the...*7 Biblical Principles for the dress Codes for Men.* It would seem that there is always a minister who wants to be different and unique, believing that the community is waiting for the church that gets it right with the new name or dress code.

Modernity is also challenging Baptist theology, doctrine, and polity. Again, it is my

---

[130] https://biblicalgenderroles.com/2014/07/11/7-biblical-principles-for-how-to-dress-as-a-christian-woman/

judgement, that it is an *age question*. Folks years ago, knew their theology and doctrine. These formed the foundation for their church and lifestyle. This is still true for some older adults attending smaller churches. Some leaned for salvation based on Calvinism and others favored an Arminianism theology. The answers back then seemed simple.

Today, it seems the focus is on whether scripture is 100% true or not. According to one person's response to a minister's article in a local newspaper...**If any of the Bible is untrue, the fabric of Christianity is a lie. Either the Bible is 100 percent authority or zero; it can't be in the middle.**[131] The truth is, even he does not believe or practice all the teachings and laws in either the New or Old Testament. My answer is, why can't our use of the scripture be less than 100%? We are doing this already. *Even fundamentalists will not accept or practice some Old Testament laws.* Young adults today show less interest in theology and doctrine. They are interested in music and programs that meet their needs.

---

[131] Bullied in the Bible Belt, by Gene Skipworth, page 94

Some churches have responded to these young adults with this reply...**we are not changing.**[132] **If you want to be a Baptist you must change and be like us. Today's young adults have answered with this statement... "we are not interested in being like you.**"[133]

Another issue facing churches today is interpretation. Are the words of Paul equal to, or more important than, the words of Jesus? **...Jesus says not to eat meat sacrificed to idols, but Paul says it is okay.**[134] Is the New Testament more important than the Old? According to some...**None of the Old Testament law is binding on Christians today. When Jesus died on the cross, He put an end to the Old Testament law.**[135] So, is circumcision in or out? Was immersion for baptism a Jewish practice or Christian? How a problem is approached for a solution will often

---

132

http://www.christianitytoday.com/edstetzer/2014/december/real-reasons-young-adults-drop-out-of-church.html

[133] http://www.recklesslyalive.com/12-reasons-millennials-are-over-church/

[134] https://www.jesuswordsonly.com/books/175-pauls-contradictions-of-jesus.html

[135] https://www.gotquestions.org/Christian-law.html

determine what decision is accepted and makes sense. If the ground rules for discussion are always predetermined on one scriptural interpretation, then the outcome will always be the same and change will continue to be arbitrary.

Common sense says much of the Old Testament does not apply to the world today because culture and laws forbid its application. Women are not owned by fathers and husbands. Marriage today is not always a religious event...**Here's the thing: the heart of the wedding ceremony is not a religious event. The core of the ceremony is the vow.** [136]

Living in a particular community should not necessarily mean that the largest church or faith group with the majority, sets the standards and rules. If there is to be any acceptance of differences, there has to be give and take, cooperation and tolerance. I'll use the example of smoking in public buildings as an example. Smokers fought for the last puff and

---

[136] https://www.quora.com/How-can-two-atheists-get-married-without-a-religious-ceremony

lost...**Smokers cost their employers nearly $6,000 a year more than staff who don't smoke.**[137] Common sense, health issues and legal battles took over the discussion; if you smoke today you are in the minority and if you do it, it is done in your own home or outside of public buildings. The rules change whether you want them to or not. If you are not in the solution, then all you can do is complain?

Religious issues fall into the same category. Sectarian prayers in school public events, religious holidays and using a bible for oaths of office can no longer be required in multicultural communities. Can these issues be a place to start a discussion for more tolerance? Why does it have to be fixed, unchanging and sectarian because that is the way it has always been? The facts are that Baptists are no longer the majority in most public issues, if atheists, agnostics, unbelievers, people of color and other religions are factored into the numbers...**when religion and politics ride in the same cart, the**

---

[137] https://www.nbcnews.com/health/health-news/smoking-employees-cost-6-000-year-more

whirlwind follows.[138] Of course, numbers matter. Especially in discussions about public safety, human welfare, and human rights, where all citizens and tax payers should have equality and justice. Let's be fair, every new generation has its traditions, so all age divisions need to be included...**nostalgia makes people feel more optimistic, it still has its place in religion.**[139] It is an emotion for feeling for the good times from the past. Reality, modernity, progressiveness and all things new are not always antagonistic attitudes, aimed at religion. Hasn't Santa Claus, Christmas trees and Easter egg hunts made their way into the church? Let's start with discussions about working together in the public arena, for issues like Christmas displays, and keep nostalgia for the lawn at church.

Public debate becomes narrowed after religious interpretations are factored into an

---

[138] https://www.futurist.com/articles-archive/religion-and-public-policy/
[139] https://www.psychologytoday.com/blog/ulterior-motives/201311/what-does-nostalgia-do

issue…**If they want to get their point across to many people they need not, it seems, have one way of speaking in the cloister and another in the plaza.**[140]

When the discussion is burdened with tradition, personal or sectarian platforms, little is accomplished for the common good. Traditions have their place for a while, but when they are kept only to make a few happy, the discussion is far from over. Any discussion on the application of bible verses, morals, values and customs **must consider all the diversity that can be found in communities and houses of worship.**[141] To live in the modern world today, everyone must accept some compromises. I remember the words a senior member gave me when I was his minister. We were considering adding an addition on to the church. He said… *"Why don't you just leave it just as it is for now; when I am gone, go ahead and do what you want to with it."* It is doubtful, that when he was growing up,

---

[140] http://www.abc.net.au/religion/articles/religious arguments in public debate

[141] https://www.theodysseyonline.com/cultural-diversity-church

and the automobile was coming of age, that he only wanted to ride to church in an old horse and buggy. Nostalgia is okay until it only satisfies your needs and not the rest of the church and community.

Chapter 7

IS YOUR HERMENEUTIC THE PROBLEM?

When the human body stimulates the brain, it then searches for an interpretation or meaning of the stimulus. Is that red car in the parking lot my car? No, it is red, but not the right color red. Are these vegetables in the grocery fresh or not? Touch or sight may give the answer. The brain answers these requests based on stored experiences and brain methods or processes used for finding different information. The longer a single experience is repeated and imbedded in our minds, the more likely the stimulus will lead to the same answer or conclusion. If we are told enough times that an activity is wrong, then our mind will remind us that this is a right to believe and a behavior to be avoided.

Hermeneutics is that branch of theology that deals with Biblical exegesis and how a bible passage is interpreted for

understanding and application.[142] Although this definition is correct, hermeneutics is not a word or concept very popular among Baptists. Most Baptists do not like to think their opinion or viewpoint for a bible passage is an interpretation. It's easier to believe their interpretations are true because they come from faith experiences which are also true. There is nothing, inherently, wrong with testing a hermeneutic (interpretation) before you accept it.

The newest phrase today is that the media is filled with *fake news*. Fake news in religion is not new. It has been going on for centuries. If there is a need to evaluate today's news for truth, isn't it time to investigate religious hermeneutics and reevaluate truth? Is it true just because the minister says tradition says it's so? And, quoting one-liners does not make them truths to live by. *God said it, and I believe it*, is one example we should question.

If the starting point for wisdom and knowledge is that it was given from God, then

---

[142] https://en.wikipedia.org/wiki/Hermeneutics

the conclusion must be correct...**The fear of the LORD is the beginning of knowledge. Fools despise wisdom and instruction.**[143] Where does Baptist wisdom and instruction come from? Probably, 80-85% comes from seminaries, universities, Christian literature, ministers, and bible schools. **Some of these sources do not agree with each other's biblical interpretations or hermeneutics for the same bible passages.** This creates more than just discussion among a variety of Baptists...**For I have been informed...my brethren...there are quarrels among you.**[144]

Just a little over sixty years ago some Baptists churches had a practice called *closed communion*, which was held for their Baptist members only. Now, First Baptist Church has communion monthly on Sunday mornings for all who claim Christianity regardless of their membership. Second Baptist Church has theirs quarterly after a business meeting. The Independent Baptist church less than five miles away uses real wine for their communion.

---

[143] Proverbs 1:7 (NASB)
[144] 1 Corinthians 1:11-13 (NASB)

The Baptist *soul competency doctrine* used to speak loudly on this until some Baptist leaders felt churches were going too far and disagreeing with denominational wisdom and views for traditional Baptist doctrine.[145] Whose interpretation is correct?... **Now I urge you, brethren, by our Lord Jesus Christ and by the love of the Spirit, to strive together with me in your prayers to God for me, that I may be rescued from those who are disobedient in Judea, and that my service for Jerusalem may prove acceptable to the saints.**[146] In this passage from Corinthians, did Paul have a problem with the Jewish disciples in Judea or did the disciples in Judea have a problem with Paul? They were both evaluating the circumcision problem with Gentiles from their own experience.

The Jewish interpretation came from the Old Testament's long-standing tradition (The Law). Paul was sharing his new hermeneutic about what works well with the Gentiles coming

---

145

http://www.txbc.org/1997Journals/Oct1997/Oct97SoulCompetency.htm

[146] Romans 15:30-31 (NASB)

into the faith uncircumcised. Paul's approach was to reinterpret the Old Testament Law and the Jews in Judea didn't like it. He was pushing his new idea; the Jews in Judea were staying with tradition.

Today, Baptists are faced the same question...**is change needed? Will Baptists change their traditional ways for ministry, evangelism, and missions?**[147] In a recent newspaper story, a Baptist leader was quoted as saying **Christianity's ways sound strange today, but churches should stay with the same ministries even if the culture around them is changing.**[148] Everyone has their opinion, including me, but church attendees are voting with their feet saying they disagree by not coming back.

The culture of the 1950's fit well with the goals and mission for Baptists when most churches were growing. Now the culture has changed, and churches are declining. Does pushing a return to a sixty-year-old cultural

---

[147] https://baptistnews.com/article/culture-warriors-wave-white-flag-get-down-to-business/

[148] The Tennessean - Moore: Embrace Christianity's 'strangeness' - August 25, 2016, page 9A

idea made sense? **When soldiers in trouble came to me with problems, I would ask what are they doing? Their explanation usually centered around what they wanted to do, and the Army wouldn't let them. So, I ask, how is your way working out for you? Of course, their way wasn't working. Now the door was opened for discussing change.[149]** I would like to ask Baptists now, how is what you are doing working out for you? If it isn't working out like you wanted, is it time to start a discussion about changing hermeneutics?

It seems important for Baptists to pass on their experiences, theology, and doctrines, based on a premise that what they heard, or read in the past, is still true. There is a paradox here for Baptists. It is not hard for a Baptist to admit human beings are imperfect, but it is harder for them to admit that their biblical interpretations are imperfect. A friend sent me an e-mail joke that makes perfect sense for this kind of logic. It mixes a literal biblical interpretation together with public policy.[150]

---

[149] Some of my army counseling experiences
[150] E-mail, Clive Arlington, 09/23/2017

...On a single day, Washington State recently passed two laws: They are, legalizing gay marriage and marijuana. Doing the two on the same day makes perfect sense and fits in with Leviticus 20:13 which says...If a man lies with another man, they should be stoned.[151] Information learned, received, or experienced can't always be true. Baptist hermeneutics that suggests that all scriptural interpretations are true and unchanging, has to be based on false logic. Yes, Paul does say about false doctrine**...For the time will come when they will not endure sound doctrine; but wanting to have their ears tickled, they will accumulate for themselves teachers in accordance to their own desires.**[152]

But, if doctrine changes, and it has, then it must not have been perfect in the first place. Listen and think before you make decisions that apply to yesterday's doctrines for today lifestyles. An example is the application for laws written in Deuteronomy and Leviticus. It is

---

[151] Leviticus 20:13 (NASB)

[152] 2 Timothy 4:3 (NASB)

impossible to prove that theology, doctrine and oral history are perfect. There are honest hermeneutical differences in doctrine among Baptists…**The religious right's view was that the culture war changed how history was studied…The new hermeneutic approached history as cultural and not because we had bad arguments for the positions we espoused, but because we had already lost it on the…ground of hermeneutics.**[153]

In a county wide crusade, I helped organize, a Baptist evangelist said…**If you are saving money for college, give it to the expenses for this crusade and God will bless you.**[154] This is just bad theology when it guarantees God's blessing if you give money to anything. So, is the media at fault if Baptists' theology is wrong, or that Christian morals, values and opinions have changed over the last sixty years? Somebody has to be blamed and it cannot be Christians and *Baptists…or* can it?

---

[153] CHRISTIAN RESEARCH JOURNAL, volume 38, number 02 (2015)
[154] Todd County Evangelistic Crusade, Elkton, KY 1964

A minister friend accepted a call to lead a Baptist congregation in Western Kentucky. He had served as pastor for three months when it came time for communion. To his frustration, he discovered it was real wine and not grape juice in the cups. He resigned on the spot and left the church.[155] **There isn't any temptation that you have experienced which is unusual for humans. God, who faithfully keeps his promises, will not allow you to be tempted beyond your power to resist.**[156] Whose theology or doctrine was correct? **The church that took the bible literally, believing Jesus served real wine at the last supper,**[157] or the minister's denominational interpretation that Baptists must abstain from all alcohol use?

Baptists disagree doctrinally whether a minister should conduct a marriage service for any divorced person. Christians who were sprinkled and are not immersed in another denomination must be re-baptized correctly for Baptist membership...**And Peter said to**

---

[155] 1 Corinthians 5:11 (ESV)

[156] 1 Corinthians 7:13 (NASB)

[157] John 2:1-11 (KJV)

them, **"Repent and be baptized every one of you in the name of Jesus Christ for the forgiveness of your sins, and you will receive the gift of the Holy Spirit.**[158] Is the minister or the church's interpretation right or wrong? It all depends on whose hermeneutic is accepted. Baptist churches are autonomous and must decide what is right for their congregation. Religious liberty for a Baptist. Interpretation is *everything* for Baptists. Humans make errors in theology and doctrine, as do churches. Baptists scoff at Adventists, Christian Scientists, Mormons, and others who claim their scriptures are true **...False Messiahs and lying teachers are going to pop up everywhere. Their impressive credentials and dazzling performances all pull the wool over the eyes often of those who ought to know better.**[159] And yet, Baptists are offended when someone disagrees with their hermeneutic. It boils down to an old Baptist preacher's saying about

---

[158] Acts 2:38 (ESV)

[159] Mathew 24:24 (The Message)

beliefs and doubts... **Believe your beliefs and doubt your doubts, but never doubt your beliefs or believe your doubts.**[160] That is about as much of a false truism as I know.

When a Baptist believes a hermeneutic is right, then all the facts in the world will not change the interpretation. If their biblical hermeneutic backs them up, then it must not be sin for them to do it.

Baptists have made moonshine, drank it, and sold it. They have lied, stolen cows, chickens, ducks, vegetables and grains and eaten all of them. Their churches believed slavery was biblical and right and they owned slaves. Baptist men have assaulted and abused women and children in the name of religion. Others, believing a man should rule his household, have made families submissive to their will. How can you be wrong if it is what you believe? Doesn't the bible say... **The Lord helps those that help themselves?**[161] **If the Lord doesn't help...was it okay then to go**

---

[160] Author's card file

[161] This saying is not a true verse in any bible translation.

on anyway? Some Baptist churches believe religious liberty allows it.

In life, there are thousands of times when people say things just to annoy someone. Here are a few that annoy me...**You will go to hell for that!** Really...hell? Just because someone said this, is it a fact that the other person is condemned to hell? Will such a belief hold up against scripture? **...Do not speak evil against one another, brothers. The one who speaks against a brother or judges his brother, speaks evil against the law and judges the law. But if you judge the law, you are not a doer of the law but a judge.**[162]

Then, there is the person who says...**My Bible tells me**...that when two people who are not married and live together it is sin...**For with the judgment you use, you will be judged, and with the measure you use, it will be measured to you.**[163] How many of those who judge, had sexual intercourse before marriage? Some of these statements come under the topic of self-righteousness. Scripture

---

[162] James 4:11 (ESV)

[163] Matthew 7:1-2 HCSB) Bible

has something to say about this also...**Woe to you, scribes, and Pharisees, hypocrites! For you tithe mint and dill and cumin, and have neglected the weightier provisions of the law: justice and mercy and faithfulness; but these are the things you should have done without neglecting the others. "You blind guides, who strain out a gnat and swallow a camel!**[164]

One more annoyance for good measure is the one that identifies all of us guilty. It is the habit for wanting mercy for our own sins and shortcomings and justice for others who have committed the same sin. If person who knows what is right to do but does not do it, to him it is sin. This is true for your family, friends, and mine. **All the paths of the Lord are mercy and truth, to such as keep His covenant and His testimonies.**[165]

Politicians and Baptists are alike, in that both want forgiveness in a sealed indictment for sins they commit and nobody, but the Lord can open or reveal. But for everybody else's

---

[164]Matthew 23:23-24 (NASB)

[165]Psalm 25:10. (KJV)

sin, front page coverage is just fine for their misdeeds.

Hermeneutics can be tricky business, especially when you are trying to prove a point as I have done above. Good hermeneutics is sometimes hard to find because scholars and ministers, as well, have used scripture to mislead people. It is important that Baptists think more about the consequences of their statements than quoting them. Think about a truth before stating or applying it. Because a Baptist tradition exists, doesn't mean it is guaranteed, right, or cannot be improved. There might be a better way. Why do we have stay on the same path...*just* because we have always done it this way?

Chapter 8

IS BAPTIST CHRISTIANITY RIGHT FOR EVERYONE?

That chapter title is almost an oxymoron, for it assumes all Christianity its theology doctrines, polity, behaviors and attitudes about anything are alike or similar enough for all. What makes any religion think that they can determine Christianity for the United States or for the world? Well Baptists really don't believe that they can convince the whole world they are right about everything. But, if a Baptist is speaking, they do believe that those in the conversation should listen to the truth as Baptists believe it.

Baptist grandmas, for example, can sometimes be outspoken. A young teenage girl brought her boyfriend over for a visit to see her grandmother. Grandma asked the boy...**Son, are you a Baptist? No Grandma, I am sorry, I am not...I am an Episcopalian, replied the boy. Well, you should be sorry, Grandma** replied.[166] And her view is still popular among Baptists today.

There is a strong charge against the media today that the Christian religion is being persecuted.[167] It may be that Christians honestly do feel strong pressure from those who believe in the separation of church and state, as well as from atheists, agnostics, and *nons* who question religion in general. **Studies show that millions of post-war children who grew up in churches, upon becoming adults, chose not to remain or return as attendees.**[168] The easiest answer from a few Baptist pulpits is...**this is the condemnation, that light is come into the world and men loved darkness rather than light because their deeds are evil.**[169] This scripture suggests two kinds of emphasis. Forgiveness of sins, which is at the heart of Christianity, and

---

[166] Author's card file

[167] https://www.huffingtonpost.com/entry/christian-persecution-is_b_9131132.html

[168] https://careynieuwhof.com/10-reasons church-attenders-attending-less-often/

[169] John 3:19 (KJV)

evangelism as the answer to point the world toward heaven.

Back in 1959, when I was ordained, the Kentucky Baptist, their state paper, always featured articles from ministers and laity about dancing at Baptist colleges. There was an unspoken fear that young men and women would get together and do something wrong if they danced.

I served as a Baptist camp manager one summer for children and youth. I was **openly criticized for allowing mixed bathing**. The ten-and-under children really were not showering together. They were swimming together in the same pool, which was a no-no for Baptists. Today, the topics have changed from dancing and mixed bathing to abortion and gay marriage. Baptists still write letters to the editor about what they interpret as sin, by quoting bible verses to prove their point...**but sanctify Christ as Lord in your hearts, always being ready to make a defense to everyone who asks you to give an account for the hope that is in you...so that in the thing in which you are slandered and those**

who revile your good behavior in Christ will be put to shame.[170] Baptists point their fingers and their ministers preach that the world is going to hell. It is the same message since the Reformation, in Martin Luther's day.

Guilt becomes the methodology and the bible is quoted for authority. There is nothing in the bible about boys and girls swimming together in a church camp swimming pool. But this falls into that nakedness idea, that temptations lead to sin. When the church points its finger at the world, the world points back at Baptist clergy and church members practicing sexual immorality, embezzlement, drunk driving, love of money, and other sins that are found in the bible...**And why do you look at the speck in your brother's eye but to not notice the log that is in your own eye?**[171]

If Christianity is suggested as a right solution for America, why are church members not attending churches? Although annual attendance continues to decline,...**a slight**

---

[170] 1 Peter 3:15-16 (NASB)

[171] Matthew 7:1-3 (KJV)

majority of adults, 55%, are churched, though the country is almost evenly split, with 45 percent qualifying as unchurched adults.[172] These numbers only count those who attend. There are thousands of members who no longer attend. Now, the real question is, where does the fault rest for declining attendance? Is it media's persecution or is the problem that churches are no longer relevant for their culture? Grandma is not going back to a tin cup on a well for water and a toilet outside her home. Young adults are not worried about boys and girls swimming in the same pool. It is more likely the Baptist voice is now against gender equality, cultural bias, racial segregation and modernity? Young adults are staying at home and those with families go to a Methodist church.

One reason for these cultural wars is that young and middle-aged Christians are not interested in the lifestyle criticisms that Baptists use to object to social and cultural change. Paul reminds young Christians that...**with gentleness correcting those who are in**

---

[172] https://www.barna.com/research/state-church-2016

opposition, if perhaps God may grant them repentance leading to the knowledge of the truth.[173] The religious side blames everyone other than themselves for not accepting biblical answers to the world's problems. The blame game started with Adam in garden...**The woman you gave me as a companion, she gave me fruit from the tree, and yes, I ate it.**[174] If the Baptists are right, then the world must be wrong. Could the opposite possibly be true, that Baptists might be wrong on some issues and the world is might be right about a few?...**Something is wrong in the Church today. I don't say that lightly, or as someone who thrives on criticizing everyone else so as to establish my own spiritual superiority, or as some-one who is feeding on sour grapes because things aren't the way I would like them. I say it because of how many people I meet on a daily basis (with people) who are discouraged by traditional**

---

[173] 2 Timothy 2:25 (NASB)

[174] Genesis 3:12 (The Message)

church and have chosen not to attend anymore.[175]

For years, Baptists were the majority in many communities and state and local governments allowed them to make decisions for public and private morals and values. Today, white Christians are a minority and in fewer numbers nationwide. Now, the Supreme Court, Federal courts, and the U.S. Congress, are beginning to question legislation and laws written with religious interpretations, **…Christian conservatives, for more than two decades a pivotal force in American politics, are grappling with Election Day results that repudiated their influence and suggested that the cultural tide… especially on gay issues…has shifted against them.**[176] **One suggestion is that the nation changed and the church wants to live in the past.**[177]

---

[175] http://blogs.christianpost.com/christianity/something-is-wrong-with-the-church

[176] www.nytimes.com/2012/11/10/us/politics/christian-conservatives-failed-to-sway-voters.html

[177] Changing World Unchanging Church Paperback – August, 1997 David Clark (Author)

An article in a local newspaper states… **that white evangelical Protestants make up only 17% of the U.S. population, according to a year-long survey of more than 100,000 people by PRRI,**[178] **a public policy research firm that specializes in issues of faith.**[179]These statistics reveal that, twenty-four percent of Americans are unaffiliated with religion. Since 1995, this figure has increased 10 percent. **Among people ages 18-29, that number rises to almost 40 percent.**[180]

If the past is any prediction, it may already be that the unchurched outnumber regular church attendees. This will not stop the letters, nor will it change the minds and points of views for those that feel they are persecuted for their religion. White children have gone to public schools with immigrants and people of color long enough now to believe racial prejudice is unchristian. They saw people of color living Christian lifestyles without the narrow minded

---

[178] Public Policy Research Institute - Texas A&M University

[179] The Tennessean 09/9/2017 page 15A "White Christians decline, still dominate GOP"

[180] The Tennessean 9/9/2017, page 15A

judgmental views on values and morals. There are fewer and fewer ex-Baptists who are taking up the persecution issue over abortion and gay rights. For many today, leaving Baptists churches for another Christian denomination is not a difficult choice, because they are tired of fighting and defending topics and issues that are no longer relevant for the world in which they live.

Let's be honest, it wasn't until the 150th anniversary of one Baptist body in 1995 that the denomination gave a public apology for its practice of racism and segregation. And even now, most white Baptist churches in the South have only a few token Latin, African American, and mixed racial members. **A second issue among dozens of Baptist denominations today is a view that women should be married, subordinate to their husbands, bear children and not hold public or religious offices.**[181] Baptists are becoming more marginalized because of their theological views. **Most Protestant churches have**

---

[181] The Tennessean 11/18/16 - Convention split over church's first female pastor, page 3A

ordained women as ministers.[182] Southern Baptists said they will not and the reason is simple...**We believe that the Bible says that while both men and women are gifted for service in the church, the office of pastor is limited to men as qualified by Scripture.**[183] Isn't it interesting that lots of white Baptist ministers who, when they were the majority and perpetrated racism and misogyny, are now the minority and screaming media persecution. **The protesters were from other Baptist churches that disapproved of Calvary calling a woman a senior pastor. Baptist churches are independent and can hire anyone they want, but if they hire a woman, they run the risk of being disfellowshipped, kicked out of their convention.**[184] When women run for office or are tired of unwanted

---

[182] The Tennessean 11/19/17 Baptists should allow female pastors. Page 2H
183

http://www.npr.org/templates/story/story.php?storyId=1069 32178
184

http://www.npr.org/templates/story/story.php?storyId=1069 32178

sexual advances, a few pulpits quote Genesis 3:16...**Yet your desire shall be for your husband, And he shall rule over you.**[185] The Apostle Paul carried this over into the New Testament church...**Let your women be silent in the assemblies, for they are not allowed to speak, but to be in subjection, just as The Written Law also says.**[186]

There are more women today in universities earning graduate degrees than men.[187] Women today will no longer be disenfranchised. It has taken years for women to come forward and identify sexual perversion in the work place. *Men are starting to run scared because Baptist women today, who like their Catholic sisters, no longer ask for a male interpretation for their spiritual or secular life.*

It is a sad day for our country when ministers, from the pulpit, marginalize women and use the bible or historic Christianity to back-up their preaching. Whose brand of Christianity will speak for all Americans? If

---

[185] Genesis 3:16 (NASB)

[186] 1 Corinthians 14:34 Aramaic Bible in Plain English

[187] http://www.breitbart.com/tech/2017/05/08-women-are-earning-more-college-degrees-than-men

Baptist Christianity speaks for America, then some Christian groups would be excluded, like Quakers and the Salvation Army, who do not require baptism. Dozens of Baptist and non-Baptist groups do not immerse all candidates for church membership. **I heard of a megachurch that accepts new members who are not baptized at all.**[188] Catholics accept Baptist baptism, but Baptists do not accept Catholic baptism.

If Baptists were to set the standards, would women be ordained, hold leadership positions in the denomination or be allowed to work outside the home? Who would be the leaders for guiding the nation's thinking for laws governing social change, human behavior, marriage, and gender use in public toilets? Men only...I hope not. *More women are coming forward and won't be pushed back to the good old days.*

The differences, for religious groups, are so great that there could not be just one standard test that would allow all to wear the Christian

---

[188]

http://www.patheos.com/blogs/geneveith/2014/07/churches-that-dont-baptize/

title...**I appeal to you, dear brothers and sisters, by the authority of our Lord Jesus Christ, to live in harmony with each other. Let there be no divisions in the church. Rather, be of one mind, united in thought and purpose.**[189] It is a fact we must recognize that there are Christians who do not agree and will create factions among us. So it is with the Baptists, as the largest non-Catholic body, if you believe the numbers. Not all Christians fall into this category. Thousands of churches are speaking out against racism by opening doors to all ethnic groups. Likewise, a few are electing and ordaining women to leadership for churches.

Baptist polity exists from liberalism at one end to fundamentalism on the other.[190] The only hope for Christianity is that the majority will cooperatively rest somewhere in the middle. Liberals and Conservatives alike quote the Constitution or the Bill of Rights when they support their views and, if they do not, neither document is mentioned.

---

[189] 1 Corinthians 1:10 (NLT)

[190] https://Baptiststoday.org/conservatisim-and-liberalism-review-by-fisher-humphreys/

Congress gets little done these days. Would it help congress if all Christian doctrines were mixed into the discussion? Baptists really value independence more than they do working together. A few Christians would rather take a chance on their independence than come together to guide a community. This is the real world. Or as some say, it is what it is. get used to it.

There is a distinctive group of doctrines and polities for Baptists, a sort of Baptist recipe... Although some of those ingredients are part of the recipe for other Christian groups, no other Christian group has the same combination of beliefs and practices as Baptists do.[191]

Communion is one example. Paul references that there were some who are unworthily taking advantage of this moment in time. He states...**If you give no thought...about the broken body of the Master when you eat and drink, you're**

---

[191]

https://www.Baptistdistinctives.org/resources/articles/what-makes-a-Baptist-a-Baptist/

running the risk of serious consequences. That's why so many of you even now are listless and sick and others have gone to an early grave.[192] I have seldom found quoting scripture was a good reason to prove your point. What a person believes about communion is their belief. Who you are seems more important to me than what you say you are...**someone will say, you have faith, and I have works. Show me your faith without your works, and I will show you my faith by my works.**[193]

When the Ten Commandments were being posted in county court houses, I took a stand against it. I stated my opinion when the county commissioners met. After the meeting, an elderly woman, stopped me, looked me straight in the eye and stated, *"Someday you will split hell wide open."* She stood her ground. I stood mine. I wasn't afraid, but glad she did not have a pistol, she might have sent me on early...**Put on the full armor of God, so that you will be**

---

[192] I Corinthians 11:29-30 (The Message)
[193] James 2:18 (NKJV)

able to stand firm against the schemes of the devil.[194] People will fight and die to prove someone is wrong and they are right. A man stated that he believed God was on his side in the Civil War. President Lincoln is said to have responded... **Sir, my concern is not whether God is on our side; my greatest concern is to be on God's side, for God is always right.**[195] Today, the real question is, whose god are we talking about?

Almost daily, somewhere in the world, there are deaths caused by a difference in strongly-held religious beliefs. Sometimes it is ethnic, tribal or political. The chaplaincy taught me a lot about religious differences for service men, women and their families. The first and most important thing I learned is that faith was usually personal, not public. When practiced within rules for behavior, it builds character. Those who had faith didn't demonstrate it in the public domain. Some of those who did shout it, didn't convince me their lifestyle would work

---

[194] Ephesians 6:11 (NASB)

[195]

https://www.brainyquote.com/quotes/quotes/a/abrahamlin388944.html

in the military. I worked with a few Baptists who were Conscientious Objectors and couldn't kill another human being. Then I worked with some who felt God's call to destroy the godless enemies of Christianity. I suggested with this last bunch, that there were Germans, Japanese, and North Koreans, who were Christians. Was God on their side or ours?

In my opinion, Christianity works best in two situations. First, it should be personal to help you build a better life for yourself as a human being. Then, it should be communal when you gather together with others who want to help and strengthen each other to build a better world...**There is no salvation offer here, just as there is no damnation. There is only acceptance.**[196]

According to the Constitution, there will be no religious test for public office. Yet, some Baptists believe if you are not at least a Protestant, then you are not qualified for public office...**Honor everyone. Love the brotherhood. Fear God. Honor the**

---

[196] Pacific Standard - The Compulsion - December/January 2018- page 13

Emperor.[197] For some, this must mean that Mormon's, Buddhists, Catholics, Seventh-Day Adventists, and Agnostics shouldn't be elected to public office. In 1962, morning prayer in public schools became a national issue. **In 2011, 65% still believed it was okay to have Christian prayers in schools.**[198]

An ardent Baptist asked me why I wouldn't support Christian prayers at public events. I asked him if the majority/minority numbers were reversed would he be satisfied with a Muslim or Hindu invoking their gods and saints be acceptable for your school children? He replied...**no, because I'm Christian, I don't believe their crap.**[199] This kind of behavior is self-righteousness for...**I want what I want, when, I want it. If you want the something different...I am sorry, but you can't have your way because your beliefs are wrong.**[200]

I am in total agreement with Baptists believing and practicing for themselves what

---

[197] 1 Peter 2:17 Holman Christian Standard Bible

[198] https://en.wikipedia.org/wiki/School_prayer

[199] Author's card file - Prayer/ 04/92

[200] https://bible.org/seriespage/lesson-9-damnable-sin-self-righteousness-romans-21-5

they believe. In my view, there will never be agreement for all. If the majority religion can always practice their beliefs at the exclusion of all others, there is little hope for diversity and cooperation on greater more important issues. There is room for all, as long as it is personal and private and not in violation of public law and safety.

Witches can have bonfires and the Afro-Cuban religion can sacrifice chickens in accordance with public law and safety.[201] Before readers get to upset, we must remember that the Old Testament laws for stoning and early European laws for hanging, drawing and quartering those who disagreed with the King, are no longer enforceable. It may be okay to remove a religious member from attending when behavior violates church or group law, but killing is prohibited in the United States.

Finally, in my opinion, as much as Christians may disagree with humanists, agnostics, and atheists over religious issues,

---

[201] http://www.nytimes.com/1993/06/12/us/supreme-court-animal-sacrifice-court-citing-religious-freedom-voids-ban-animal.html

both sides need to understand that personal beliefs will have some influence on personal decisions but cannot and should not be used for denial for purchasing goods and services in the public domain.

If your particular sect or religion wants to deal only with its members, they should be allowed. However, once a business is opened to the public it should not be able to deny service to any person who is religious or non-religious. My recommendation is that we let churches be churches in whatever doctrine, theology, and polity they hold scripturally true. Let them be independent and practice their denominational doctrines and religious liberty. Winston Churchill said this in January 1912...**Each generation seeks and demands harmony in the relations of life, harmony between religion, science, history and government. It is becoming increasingly apparent, for example, in spite of any seeming indications to the contrary, that a civilization cannot hold at the same time a**

pre-reformation idea of the Church and a post-reformation idea of government.[202]

202

www.theatlantic.com/magazine/archive/1912/01/modern-government-and-christianity/376203/

Chapter 9

BAPTIST DOCTRINE - DOES IT REALLY SPEAK FOR GOD?

I want to begin with two simple definitions: Theology is...**the field of study and analysis of God's attributes and relations to the universe; study of divine things or religious truth; divinity.**[203] And doctrine relates to theology and is **a particular principle, position, or policy taught or advocated, as of a religion.**[204] Of course we should agree that religious doctrine comes from a theological interpretation of holy scripture. Doctrine is how Baptist theology is applied in daily life and that is where the battle lines are drawn. For Baptists, theology may be an issue, but doctrine is the big problem. Baptists generally only argue theology in seminaries and universities. Having served as a minister, chaplain, denominational leader and taught in universities, there is little interest

---

[203] http://www.dictionary.com/browse/theology
[204] http://www.dictionary.com/browse/doctrine

in discussing theology. Baptists today, are more interested in politics and governing women's health and gender issues, public restroom use, and modernity. Jesus came as a Jew and spoke and taught mostly to Jews about Jewish laws, daily life, and the hereafter. While he interacted with Gentiles, his main focus was with the Jews about a different and better understanding of God's promises to Israel. Many years later, Paul also came as a Jew; spoke about guidelines and behaviors for Jews and Gentiles in newly formed groups and congregations today called a church.

Sometimes Baptists resemble the Pharisees in the New Testament; rigid, unchanging and demanding obedience to the doctrines. **In my view, Baptists spend too much time interpreting and applying Paul's writings.**[205] They were written to early believers who were without any Christian history to guide them. He gave them his interpretation for the new faith. Everything in Paul's letters can't be applicable for theology, doctrine and church polity in today's churches.

---

[205] http://www.problemswithpaul.com/

You do not have to agree with me on this, but ask yourself...*is my church practicing everything Paul wrote or said as guidelines written to a particular New Testament church?* Your answer is probably no, we do not do everything. Therefore, all scripture that is inspired and not believed and/or practice makes scripture questionable. Remember the 100% statement that it must be all true or none of it, as quoted about in Chapter 6?

Luke shows there was a togetherness in the early church...**These all with one mind were continually devoting themselves to prayer, along with the women, and Mary the mother of Jesus, and His brothers.**[206] However, the longer the early church survived the more complicated and uncooperative it became among Christians, Jews, and Gentiles. Early Christianity struggled to find a form that would include theology and doctrines that were favorable to everyone in the faith. Among the many schisms in early church history, the majority come over doctrinal disagreements. It is interesting to look at some of the writings that

---

[206] Acts 1:14 (NASB)

are apocryphal and were not selected for the New Testament. **They show a variety of theologies, doctrines, and polity that were used by early groups who called themselves Christians.**[207]

Paul's letters to young Timothy are filled with advice for the young inexperience pastor **…Pay close attention to yourself and your teaching; persevere in these things, for as you do this you will ensure salvation both for yourself and for those who hear you.**[208] In his letters he calls himself an apostle. **No other New Testament author uses this word for themselves as a term for authority or the perfect example for a Christian church member.**[209] The advice to his Corinthian church, filled with problems, was…**I exhort you therefore, be imitators of me.**[210] So, is todays goal for the church to replicate Paul's wisdom as intended for these early churches? If this is true, let's admit then, that it will be

---

207

https://en.wikipedia.org/wiki/New_Testament_apocrypha

[208] 1 Timothy 4:16 (NASB)

[209] http://www.problemswithpaul.com/

[210] 1 Corinthians 4:16 (NASB)

impossible to replicate any of these early churches, for there is no one model or standard that fits all unless you believe every one of Paul's interpretations is applicable to churches today. Paul wrote instructions that applied specific problems for a single church which may or may not need application for all his churches. No church that I know of takes every word from Paul as gospel and applies it to themselves. Like good Baptists, we pick and choose the verses and words carefully, so we can apply them where we think it supports our point of view.

All this is good for some churches, but not all churches. Think about this? Are there guidelines that you can think of where one interpretation applies to all? As a Baptist, would it be sensible to say Paul's doctrine must be used in all churches that carry the name Baptist? I do not think there would be but a few that agree!

What standards did New Testament churches have back then. Each one had something different? They may have had good results, but would those same doctrines work today? I cannot name a Baptist church that forces women into a single hair style, or dress requirement. I have heard of a few churches that do not permit women to pray in public worship or teach men in bible study. I know only one minister who teaches that women are not to speak in church without their husband's permission. Are any of these churches growing? Is there a large majority among Baptists who look to these ministers and their churches to set the standards for all other Baptists churches? Will these theological and doctrinal interpretations change cultures? Finally, are young adults convinced Baptist doctrine and polity are the right values, morals, and behaviors to answer life's challenges for today?

Christianity has very little resemblance to its early beginnings. Theologians have made their fame and history attacking ancient interpretations they disagreed with. **It is a fact that doctrine is still changing today, and maybe faster than in the early church**[211] There was little agreement back then among

---

[211] https://lifehopeandtruth.com/change/the-church/was-christianity-designed-to-evolve/

leaders, churches, and believers concerning what was important or official.

Martin Luther broke away from the Roman church, taking away the authority for books in the Apocrypha located between the New and Old Testaments stating...**these are book(s) which are not held equal to the Sacred Scriptures and yet are useful and good for reading.**[212] Most Protestants took the Apocrypha out altogether when printing their bibles. John Calvin took a different view of Martin Luther's position for scripture with his Thirty-Nine Articles to establish the **Church of England doctrine.**[213] Some Baptists today still favor **Calvinism over Arminianism for doctrine.**[214]

Are the words of Paul equal to, or more important than, the words of Jesus? Most Baptists would say no, they are not, but they will quote Paul more often than Jesus to prove a point of view or give their opinion especially

---

[212] http://goodnewspirit.com/apocrypha.htm

[213] http://www.britainexpress.com/History/tudor/39articles.htm

[214] https://www.huffingtonpost.com/2013- Calvinism- is dividing the southern Baptist convention.

when it relates to daily living and lifestyles. Paul's comment on the differences between men and women's hairstyle was identified with the secular world...**Does not even nature itself teach you that if a man has long hair, it is a dishonor to him, but if a woman has long hair, it is a glory to her: for her hair is given her for a covering.**[215] Women's hairstyles today are not going to one style. Baptist ministers are wise not to go there.

Baptists today have little interest about how the bible's books were finally selected. The largest and longest debate today has been over scripture's authority and whether the bible is inspired and without error. A verse, often quoted, is...**All scripture is given by inspiration of God, and is profitable for doctrine, for reproof, for correction, for instruction in righteousness:**[216] What is interesting to me is that Paul's quote here wasn't about the New Testament at all. For it wasn't totally written, collected or approved as scripture; for use until years later. How could

---

[215] 1 Corinthians 11:14-15 (NASB)
[216] 2 Timothy 3:16 (KJV)

Paul write or approve the New Testament as inspired doctrine? He most certainly meant the Old Testament, which he did know...**What shall we say, then? Is the law sinful? Certainly not! Nevertheless, I would not have known what sin was had it not been for the law.**[217]

Paul knew the law, but not the four gospels, for some hadn't been written or circulated yet. Doctrine, since Paul's time, has undergone change and will continue to go through changes...**and my message and my preaching were not in persuasive words of wisdom, but in demonstration of the Spirit and of power, so that your faith would not rest on the wisdom of men, but on the power of God.**[218]

Preaching was and is important for laity to grow spiritually in word and deed. And great preaching challenges those in the pew to grow in grace and service and do like the early disciples...**All the believers were one in heart and mind. No one claimed that any of**

---

[217] Romans 7:7-8 (NASB)
[218] 1 Corinthians 2:4-5) (NASB)

their possessions was their own, but they shared everything they had. With great power the apostles continued to testify to the resurrection of the Lord Jesus. And God's grace was so powerfully at work in them all that there were no needy persons among them. and put it at the apostles' feet, and it was distributed to anyone who had need.[219]

Baptist Sunday School material is heavy on Baptist doctrine, selecting passages to show what is right for a Christian's lifestyle...**Now flee from youthful lusts, and pursue righteousness, faith, love and peace with those who call on the Lord from a pure heart.**[220] This advice is good, but how it is interpreted for daily living's do's and don'ts is the problem. Which leads to...**foolish and ignorant speculations, knowing that they produce quarrels.**[221]

It takes maturity, education, and lots of language skills to hold a discussion that leads

---

[219] Acts 4:32-35 (NIV)
[220] 2 Timothy 2:22 (NASB)
[221] 2 Timothy 2:23 (NASB)

to truth, enlightenment, and trust in scripture. Few Baptists, ministers included, are willing or able to lead in a doctrinal discussion for the good of all. Paul's man-made doctrines and guidelines were for a particular time and place. Preaching, study and discussions should be held to make a point...**But avoid foolish controversies, genealogies, dissensions, and quarrels about the law, for they are unprofitable and worthless.**[222]

I think it is quite humorous that those who quote Paul for defense of their doctrine, avoid Paul's warning about fruitless discussions when trying to prove a point of view. *The purpose of a discussion should be for building relationships, creating information for fruitful thought and exploration. It isn't a time to build a platform to prove superior wisdom or intellectual ability.* Worthy discussion builds up and does not destroy a person by using guilt and proof-texting scriptures. Doctrine has been debated and argued continually over the centuries among Christians, Jews, Catholics

---

[222] Titus 3:9 (NASB)

and Protestants with little success or real convincing proof.

One of the best examples of quibbling differences for doctrinal interpretations is to add *end-of-times apocalypticism* to any discussion. Apocalypticism is the doctrinal study for the millennial reign of Jesus Christ and the end of the world as we know it. What are the signs for His return? Who will come with Him? Who will reign with him? Who are those who will be destroyed and forced to honor His return? And on and on go the questions.

Each theologian has his or her own interpretation for prophetic scriptures. Then, there are those who mix some of their own views with other theologians. David Meade, a self-proclaimed bible researcher, claimed Christ's return would be September 23, 2017. **When that date passed he amended his new date to the middle of October which didn't happen either.**[223] There are charts, drawings, grafts, and paintings depicting particular verses. Ministers will argue their points of view;

---

[223] The Week Magazine 10/6/2017 page 6

using Greek and Hebrew word etymologies to win debates. What does all this prove if those who need it are not attending?

Moses warned about when a religious leader makes prophetic statements about the future and the prophecy turns out to be untrue...**a prophet who presumes to speak in my name anything I have not commanded, or a prophet who speaks in the name of other gods, is to be put to death.**[224] This is one standard ministers do not want enforced.

If Baptists cannot agree on their doctrine, why is this an issue for removing tenured Baptist professors, firing pastors, kicking churches out of associations, and denominations when they disagree and are just acting like Baptists? Yes, Baptist believe in religious liberty, until you disagree with them. As a result, hundreds, even thousands have suffered because doctrine was made more important than people.

224

https://www.biblegateway.com/passage/?search=Deuteronomy+18:20-22

Why make enemies of other Christians? **Jesus said...Love your enemies, do good to those who hate you, bless those who curse you, pray for those who mistreat you. If someone slaps you on one cheek, turn to them the other also. If someone takes your coat, do not withhold your shirt from them. Give to everyone who asks you, and if anyone takes what belongs to you, do not demand it back. Do to others as you would have them do to you.**[225]

Since it is customary for Baptists to pick and choose what doctrines to believe and practice, why do they expect non-Baptists to believe and obey them? If religious liberty is right for all Baptists, it must be right for Catholics, Seventh Day Adventists, Mormons, Muslims, Jews, and all other bible-based faith groups.

How can any denomination believe their doctrine speaks for God to the exclusion of other faiths? Baptist doctrine, at its best, is man-made. Sadly, this is just what they do and then wonder why a statement made by a

---

[225] Luke 6:27-36 (NIV)

college student at a Billy Graham meeting ...
"Jesus Christ I can accept, it is Christians I can't stand,"[226] is still relevant today.

---

[226] Billy Graham Crusade, Knoxville, TN 1970

Chapter 10

WHO SHOULD MARRY, AND NOT MARRY?

I have always had an interest in problem-solving. Serving in a military environment led me to believe that solving problems was not something that you just discussed and quoted a passage out of an old military handbook. Commanders ask their staffs to look beyond past wars, tactics, weapons, and strategies for battle plans to fight today's wars. No solution is better than any other until it is tested.

With this simple introduction, let's look at Baptist discussions on marriage. The first issue is the old and new cultural view of women. In 2016 a Baptist seminary professor, speaking at a single women's conference, stated in his opinion, women who refuse to marry and bear children are out of God will. I do not know if the professor was interpreting Paul's words to Timothy which said...**Women, however, will be saved through child-bearing, if they continue in faith, love, and holiness, with**

self-control,[227] or what Moses wrote in an earlier bible verse that is often quoted by parents who want grandchildren...**And God blessed them. And God said to them, Be fruitful and multiply and fill the earth and subdue it.**[228] So, are marriages assumed, required or arranged and if so, according to whom for what purpose?

Now we have several opinions and bible verses. My thinking is, we are at the same place we started: opinions about women marriage and childbearing. We heard from an educated seminary professor, an ancient Jewish leader, an early Christian church planter, and grandparents wanting children. All want to give advice for marriage and tell women what to do and how to live in the modern world. Mix in with these some conservative male clergy's opinions, add some old worn out traditions about women and what you have are impossible, impractical and unreasonable suggestions. The world is changing, and men and parents no longer

---

[227] 1 Timothy 2:15 BSB)
[228] Genesis 1:28 (ESV)

legally can decide, the requirements, for what adult women will or won't do. With this rather biased solution, it is interesting that the discussion totally leaves out the women.

Rather than looking in scripture for reasons for marriage or asking men what women should do, wouldn't it be wise to include women in the discussion? Paul, like many men today have decided that women are property and should submit to a husband's will about everything...**Likewise also women should adorn themselves in respectable apparel, with modesty and self-control, not with braided hair or gold or pearls or costly clothing, but with what is becoming to women, professing the fear of God through good works.**[229]Women today are refusing to listen to men setting the rules about their careers, childbearing, or what lifestyles they can or cannot choose.

Having started with the women's issue, let's move on to current information about marriage. There are workable solutions that can improve the averages for loving, lasting marriages.

---

[229] 1 Timothy 2:15 BSB)

Some believe that statistical evidence makes a better case. I say, not always, but let's look at some figures. **Depending on who is counting and how the totals are determined, marriage statistics, show there is about a 50-50 chance for success.**[230] It is important to factor into today's facts that men and women are choosing not to marry early because success is unlikely for their economic, political, racial, gender, or lifestyle reasons.

One reason is…**Women who were born in the 1980s and 1990s are on track to stay unmarried at rates much higher than previous generations. In fact, the marriage rate for women currently in their early 30s is close to zero. By the time women born in the 1940s reached the age of 23, only 25 percent of them remained unmarried. Now…for unmarried women born in the 1990's, it is 81 percent.**[231] Marriage and divorce figures do not include singles waiting until later, the unhappily married, separated

---

[230] http://www.divorcesource.com/ds/main/u-s-divorce-rates-and-statistics-1037.shtml

[231] http://www.businessinsider.com/heres-why-millennials-arent-choosing-to-get-married

married couples and those who are not married but living together. We live today in a world Paul never knew. **Paul's ideas for marriage may have been right for the times, but his guidance, when applied today, will cause problems.**[232] **If more and better information is factored into marriage, then the odds for success should go up.**[233]

Now, there are all kinds of reasons for conducting weddings. Baptists choose theirs, others faith groups who conduct or arrange marriages have different reasons and standards. Today, most want to start with the word *love*. Love is an emotion; not always the best qualifying factor for marriage. I have known couples who loved each other, but couldn't live happily ever after, on just love...**Love bears all things, believes all things, hopes all things, endures all things. Love never ends.**[234] This is spiritually a

---

232

http://www.christianitytoday.com/edstetzer/2014/february/marriage-divorce

[233] https://www.psychologytoday.com/blog/the-joint-adventures-well-educated-couples/201206/key-factors-impact-your-odds-marital-success

[234] 1 Corinthians 13:7-8 (NASB)

wonderful, and a very romantic passage. Couples have used these words for years in their weddings vows; but, the words didn't save their marriage. Biblical love is not enough for the times in which we live. **There are as many divorces among religious couples as there are in non-religious.**[235] Religious views for biblical marriage are untestable because no two people or two marriages use the same morals and values.

Marriage is complicated and if you honestly add a rapidly-changing culture, you are asking people to sign a contract for sixty-plus years that is nearly impossible to keep. Who knows what it will be like to raise hers, his, or their children in a blended marriage, ten years from now. Is it possible to provide for a marriage and family today with only one adult working? Too many questions asked and guesses for answers.

Yes, adults are waiting longer to make the marriage commitment. More and better information helps couples take a longer look

---

[235] https://www.focusonthefamily.com/about/focus-findings/marriage/divorce-rate-in-the-church-as-high-as-the-world

before marriage. Still, there are other issues that must be factored into marriage that will come after the vows. A nice young couple came into the church where I served and asked if I could perform their wedding service. They had chosen to come to me to discuss their wedding plans because the church that they were attending wouldn't allow their pastor to marry anyone who was divorced. Scripture says...**Whoever divorces his wife and marries another woman commits adultery against her.**[236]

The biblical issue here comes under the heading of *church doctrine*. The church's doctrine stated that no wedding could be performed in the church by a minister if either person was divorced. Their minister, in refusing to perform the service, did tell them that they could return, after marriage, and become church members. What he didn't tell them was that if they became members they could not hold an elected office because he was divorced, and she was married to a man who failed the scripture marriage test. **That's**

---

[236] Mark 10:11(NASB)

it…talents wasted, leadership never used, but they could give their tithes and offerings when the plates were passed.[237] Maybe this fits in with Pauls' warning…**if they cannot control themselves, they should marry, for it is better to marry than to burn with passion.**[238]

Religious rules and marriage traditions can be destructive. The *way it was back then* is not the way it is today. Nor, will it be the same in the future. White wedding dresses, brides who throw flowers at hopeful young women or a drunken bachelor party is not the point I am making. Weddings can be anywhere, last longer, and stay happier than those in a church. Expensive weddings do not guarantee a long happy marriage. I heard this story about my Baptist minister's daughter's wedding. On her wedding night the groom threw his pants at his new bride and asked, "*Are you was going to wear them?*" She declined; and then he replied that he would. It turned out the groom's grandfather had told this story about himself

---

[237] http://www.bible-teaching-about.com/divorced.html
[238] 1 Corinthians 7:9 (NIV)

and now the grandson though it was a tradition. Rigid scriptural interpretations are another mistake. Traditions should be few and far between. Every couple should make their own.

A man came to me and asked if I would make an appointment for him with his ex-wife. I talked to her and we made the appointment. He came with his second wife and their six-year-old son. He and his new wife, after their marriage, joined a very fundamental Baptist church. And, under the preaching of their minister, discovered that he could not go to heaven having two living wives. Under the advice of their minister if all parties were willing, he should divorce his second wife that God didn't recognize anyway and provide support for her and their child. Then he must remarry his first wife. They could live apart if she had her own financial support. If not, then he must support her also.

Do you want to guess how this discussion went? Not well. Finally, after 40 minutes I gave him this solution…*Pray to God every day that you will outlive your first wife or second wife by a few minutes. If you do, you eliminate the condition that keeps you from heaven, for at the time of your death a few minutes later you only had one wife.* Everyone left the meeting satisfied. His first wife didn't have to get married to him again. The first husband knew all he had to do was live longer than his first wife or the second wife...**For the married woman is bound by law to her husband while he is living; but if her husband dies, she is released from the law concerning the husband.**[239] I suppose the same is true if both wives died first. Please, believe me, I did not invent either of these two stories.

As a minister in Florida I was asked if I would officiate a wedding service for an elderly couple who wanted to be married in the eyes of God, but who would not have a State of Florida marriage license...**Thou shall not bear false witness.**[240] Their reasoning was simple. The man's income came from a small monthly social security check. The woman's income came from her deceased husband's pension. If she legally married again she lost this pension. Together with their combined incomes of less

---

[239] Romans 7:2 (NASB)
[240] Romans 13:1-13 KJV

158

than $700, they could live in an old mobile home. Separated, neither had enough income to pay for a second mobile home, rental space, utilities and food. Neither own an automobile or had other financial resources. I married them and didn't advertise this wedding knowing...**Let every person be in subjection to the governing authorities. For there is no authority except from God, and those which exist are established by God.**[241] I knew that I would be criticized, by some, for failing to obey scripture. This scriptural interpretation wasn't mine. So, why criticize me for putting two wonderful elderly Christian people together? They who knew each other and their diseased spouses for years?

I chose to follow the words of Jesus...**And the King will say, 'I tell you the truth, when you did it to one of the least of these my brothers and sisters, you were doing it to me.**[242] Who wants to tell them God won't bless their Christian marriage and home because

---

[241] Romans 13:1 (NASB)

[242] Matthew 25:40 (TLT)

they didn't have a Florida marriage license? **Which is the better choice? Legalism, that criticizes two people for living together without a Florida marriage license,**[243] or common sense? Two Christian people living together, married in their faith, supporting each other with love and the approval of their friends and family?

It isn't the words, rules, or counseling before the marriage that will make a marriage last. Success in any relationship begins when a person grows up learning that he or she must be responsible for themselves in the world in which they live and the situations they create. *If in choosing to marry a person of the same gender, or different race, religion or culture, responsibility rests then with both persons, which in my opinion, overrides love, ancient traditions and religious rules.* When divorce is easy, and it is, it opens the door for anything that makes a person unhappy. Making divorce harder to get won't save marriages. If responsible people agree on a marriage, then

---

[243] https://bible.org/seriespage/lesson-57-why-jesus-hates-legalism-luke-1137-54

whatever decisions they agree on, their chances for success in the future, should be better. And if they can't agree, divorce should not be a black mark on their lives.

Life is filled with experiences that do not work out as well as intended. Take responsibility for all your actions and behaviors. Learn from your mistakes. Be mature, do what is right even if divorce comes, there is a way to do what is best for all. It is a truism that... *no one is perfect*.

There are solutions that can build better marriages, if people will take responsibility for their actions and churches will quit trying to run people's lives with requirements and criticism. When churches keep adding rules to marriages in changing times, it only adds more imperfect information into an already difficult subject. Marriage is a difficult subject. Maybe it is time to get a group together and start a discussion for your church.

Chapter 11

WHY BAPTISTS CAN'T SOLVE THE RESTROOM QUESTION

Let's be honest, most Baptists have a problem with sex or something related to sex and it is not just biological. Discussions about sex can be serious and sometimes humorous. Any sex discussion may have a couple hundred different interpretations, definitions and usages depending on who, what, when, and how the subject is presented. The word *sex* is seldom used by Baptists with a positive connotation in sermons, literature or public discourse.

Until Baptists are willing to admit that they are a part of the problem, they will seldom be involved in working toward viable solutions. Scripture says...**God created man ...male and female he created them. And God blessed them and said be fruitful and multiply.**[244] That's it! Sex is good and has God's approval. Now, the problem is ours to

---

[244] Genesis 1:27-28 (NASB)

solve on how we see if sex is good for anything other than procreation. For Baptists, sex encompasses topics on what they want and expect for humanity.

Baptists are no different from other religious groups or cultures who put a different interpretation or spin on whether any purpose can be for good or evil. Now the Tennessee-based Council for Biblical Manhood and Womanhood declared that they were taking a stand that transgender self-conception is a sin. **And so, gay marriage, according to the article, is contradictory to the roles God intended.**[245] It seems obvious to this group that the biblical statement…**He created him; male and female He created them,**[246] seems simple enough for everyone to understand.

But, Baptists don't just stop there. This interpretation doesn't end with male and female gender. It now includes which genders can marry, use the same public restroom and when should a woman obey state law and abandon a physician's health advice. Abortion

---

[245]The Week Magazine 9/2/2017, page 12
[246] Genesis 1:27 (NASB)

may be bad but, Baptists can't agree whether some circumstances should allow it. It's the same disagreements that exist over what is right about sex inside a marriage, between consenting adults and whether Planned Parenthood should be outlawed. I am not the first one to tell Baptists this statement...*that the world really doesn't care what they think about sex for themselves or others.* That said, it doesn't solve the problem or get a sensible discussion going to work on solutions for a better community.

Certainly, procreation is a valid reason. And yet, some Christian groups are strongly against In Vitro Fertilization. This is an old over-used mantra ..."*Yes, you can do it, but you can only do it the way we say you can.*" Sexual relations are not one dimensional nor does it have just one purpose. Scripture provides us with many examples of sex gone wrong and unpunished. Look up...**The 6 Raunchiest, Most Depraved Sex Acts From the Bible**[247] **Sex in the Old Testament stories reveals cultural**

---

[247] http://www.cracked.com/article_16546_the-6-raunchiest-most-depraved-sex-acts-from-bible

interpretations that are no longer enforceable under United States or most Western legal statues.[248] **Deuteronomy lists dozens of guidelines, rules, and laws concerning sexual morals and values relating to communal life, marriages and the spoils of war.**[249] Applications were simple...**Show no pity: life for life, eye for eye, tooth for tooth, hand for hand, foot for foot**[250]**Then, punishments were different and depended on whether you were an Israelite, slave, a stranger, man or woman.**[251]

Enforcement is impossible for these scriptures, which leads many to question modern applications for what was written in

---

[248] https://www.biblestudytools.com/topical-verses/bible-verses-about-sex/

[249] https://theopolisinstitute.com/the-death-penalty-in-the-mosaic-law/

[250] Deuteronomy 19:21 (RSV)

251

https://blogs.ancientfaith.com/departinghoreb/understanding-violence-old-testament-part-prisoners-war-forced-marriage/ **And**
http://religion.oxfordre.com/view/10.1093/acrefore/9780199340378.001.0001/acrefore-9780199340378-e-45

the Old Testament.[252] The next question should be, *whose interpretation is correct for enforcement by methods other than stoning?*...**But if this charge is true, that the girl was not found a virgin, she shall be brought to the door of her father's house and there the men of her town shall stone her to death.**[253]

Let's be realistic. How many Baptist men and women were virgins on their wedding day? What would the size of this problem be today if only virgins could marry, and non-virgins were stoned to death? Baptists and some other religions have a sex problem, first with women, then gays, lesbians, and finally transgender men, women, and children. Baptists are uneasy about discussing restrooms and gender. Here is a simple solution from the Old Testament, when there were no bathrooms in Israel...**Designate a place outside the camp where you can go to relieve yourself. As part of your equipment have something to**

---

[252] https://questions.org/tag/mosaic-law/

[253] Deuteronomy 22:21-22 (NASB)

dig with, and when you relieve yourself, dig a hole and cover up your excrement.[254]

Does this simple solution apply to today's world? Hardly! So much for quoting bible verses and making them apply to people who do not live in an Old Testament world. Baptists leave this verse out for discussion and choose others.

When cultures change laws and rules, sometimes religious groups and Baptists have a hard time accepting or adjusting to change. Especially if the subject is related to sex. Hollywood has given Baptist ministers hundreds of subjects to use as illustrative material for sermons on passions that lead to sexual sin...**For while we were in the flesh, the sinful passions, which were aroused by the Law, were at work in the members of our body to bear fruit for death.**[255]

The Nashville Tennessean reported on a religious antigay meeting's decision with this opinion...**the religious right's deep**

---

[254] Deuteronomy 23:10-13 (NIV)
[255] Romans 7:5 (NASB)

insecurity over its waning influence over how Americans think.[256] Do Baptists, as individuals or groups, really need to preach, shout, and make more statements about sexual differences? Is segregation, as in the Muslim world, or making women a man's property, as in old Israel, a workable solution today? If it is true, where are all the young adults and their families flocking to join churches where everything about sex is handled perfectly? When will the message from unbelievers get through to the religious right that they just don't care what churches believe about bathrooms, sex and sinful behaviors? How long will it take for the believers to accept and apply doctrine to themselves, instead of trying to force it on others?

Statistics are available and growing for internet pornography. **Yes!...this sex topic is out of control and frightening.**[257] While Baptists stand with the majority on trying to control pornography and sexual deviancy

---

[256] The Week Magazine 9/22/2017, page 12

[257] http://gizmodo.com/5552899/finally-some-actual-stats-on-internet-porn

activities, we must face some unwanted facts. Baptists also are a part of this problem. Baptist members and ministers are just as guilty for looking at pornography as any other religious or nonreligious person. That said, their most popular approach to solving the pornography problem is to shame others. **Baptists, at one time, in some states in the South, made up the largest religious prison population.**[258]

Pointing a finger at the guilty and not including yourself is hypocritical...**But I say to you, that whoever looks on a woman to lust after her has committed adultery with her already in his heart.**[259] Cleaning up church members sexual lifestyle is not the only problem Christians face. Human sexuality covers a broad spectrum of problems, and yet Baptists choose to relate it to a single doctrinal issue...**The biblical ground for free will lies in the fall into sin by Adam and Eve that occurred in their willfully-chosen disobedience to God.**[260] Those few words

---

[258] http://www.adherents.com/misc/adh_prison.html

[259] Matthew 5:28 (KJV)

[260] https://en.wikipedia.org/wiki/Free_will_in_theology

about sinful behavior cover all that is needed to use guilt as the solution for sexual problems. Ask around; is this guilt idea a working solution?

I was a minister in Florida when an elderly member of our church was found guilty of watching internet pornography and fondling his step-granddaughter. So, while awaiting trial, he wanted to continue to attend church. I agreed to work with him to help him find forgiveness and understand his situation. After some discussion with my deacons, they suggested that he go to another church.

I reminded them that if God forgives sins, why couldn't we forgive him and each other? Some still disagreed. Then I suggested in summary that what they were telling me is that if they were guilty of a sin mentioned in the bible, then I was supposed to come to them and tell them find another church. Suddenly, they all agreed he could come back to church while awaiting his trial...**Bear with each other and forgive one another if any of you has a**

grievance against someone. Forgive as the Lord forgave you.[261]

Surprisingly, when you ask most Baptists to turn their criticism around and apply it to themselves they often refuse to believe this is a good method for dealing with sinners. A double standard is alive and well in many Christian's lifestyles.

If Baptist adults do not understand sexual issues outside of religious doctrines, how is it possible that they know how to instruct children and youth to understand sex, other than making them ashamed of their gender? Baptists will never agree on sexual behavior and misconduct until they will admit that the subject must be approached with a point of view other than shame.

Male and female children use the same toilets in homes, day cares, and preschool centers. *Going to the toilet is not a sexual problem for young children, unless society makes it one.* What would be wrong with boys and girls in elementary school using the same restroom with a teacher present to send the

---

[261] Colossians 3:13 (NASB)

boys to a urinal or toilet and girls to stalls? Shocked at this approach? It happens all over the world, why not in the United States? It would solve the gender, transgender, girls' and boys' restroom problem in public schools. With a teacher present, who is going to misbehave?

Would anyone dare to suggest, that children in early grades, have not seen pornography on the internet? When times change, mature people learn to adapt and find ways to adjust. The Corinthian church had a problem with speaking in tongues. **Paul closed the chapter with this verse…And I show you a still more excellent way.**[262] This may surprise you, but adults are constantly showing and educating children with a better way to do most things. Why not begin with early toilet training and forget all this male female shaming; which gender gets to go where, thing?

If we have to find answers in scripture how about this one?…**If you then, who are evil, know how to give good gifts to your**

---

[262] 1 Corinthians 12:31 (NASB)

children, how much more will your Father who is in heaven give good things to those who ask him![263] Solving this problem is not a religious issue, it is a cultural one. Let's get started working together on this problem. It can be solved if we will cooperate on a solution.

Baptists need to get rid of a few sex-laden words like *nudity* and *nakedness*. I am told that some Christian physicians, who went to Africa in short term working groups, covered naked African women with a sheet when they came for health care exams. If the natives see no need for covering, why do the physicians?

Now, let's apply some of this to the United States. We do have nude bathing beaches and nudist colonies. There is nakedness and nudity in movies, plays, sculpture, paintings, art, and magazines. Smart parents will teach their children about the dangers of alcohol, guns and drugs. Why not teach them that nakedness and nudity also have their place in culture? Adults should not be afraid to discuss, with all children, that guns, drugs, alcohol, and sex can be dangerously misused or used appropriately

---

[263] Matthew 7:11 (English Standard Version)

depending on time and place. It helps a child to understand the problem first and then what the responsible behavior is for the right action. When parents hide their naked bodies, they teach their children to be ashamed of their gender.

It is surprising to some Baptists that it is not unusual for a child to be born...**with several variations in sex characteristics.**[264] **If Baptists believe that God is our creator then why must they have a different attitude about children who are born with mixed genitalia.**[265] Some will counter my proposal with scripture that the bible is not wrong on homosexuality. Okay, that was then. What about today? If we are all God's creation, why is there a move to segregate us according to gender differences? We do not humiliate the mental or physical handicapped this way. We can accept and integrate children born without arms and legs. Are not all God's creation?

Do we want to separate mix gendered children in worship? Baptists can take the lead

---

[264] https://en.wikipedia.org/wiki/Intersex
[265] https://www.gotquestions.org/hermaphrodites.html

for better solutions if they wanted to do it. I believe that most Baptists, because of their Baptist upbringing are ashamed to discuss these kinds of sexual issues.

So, the accusatory language continues over who or what children might use or be seen in school restrooms. Is the best solution to examine all children at entry grade level and mark records so they can use the required restroom? Is it a good idea for children to wait until their parents are ready to discuss sex? Why wait? Schools are places for learning. Let's get with the program and ask for guidelines from teachers who can help the children learn how to deal with change.

Chapter 12

WHICH BIBLE TRANSLATION OR WHOSE INTERPRETATION IS CORRECT?

Baptists, and some other Christian groups, are prone to argue about which bible version or translation is the right one for use. My opinion is, **there are no perfect translations or scriptural interpretation that is right or correct for everyone.**[266] Each church's minister should take the lead to examine different translations and ask the congregation to help in choosing the best one for each congregation. If the leaders make this an issue, then members will feel a responsibility to follow. **All scripture is given by inspiration of God, and is profitable for doctrine, for reproof, for correction, for instruction in righteousness: That the man of God may be perfect, thoroughly furnished unto all good works.**[267]

---

[266] https://www.firstthings.com/article/2003/12/a-bible-for-everyone

[267] 2 Timothy 3:16-17 (KJV)

177

Reading from the same scripture translation helps and adds understanding for discussion and interpretation **for those in the pews or at home.**[268] This might be a good place for Christian congregations to come together. This could also help for a better understanding and agreement on doctrine and polity for a local church.

When I was ordained back in 1959, folks brought their bibles with them to church. Scriptures were read from the pulpit, and a congregation followed along using their own bibles or one provided in the pew. Similarity was common.

One Sunday, I chose to read from the _Living Bible_, and learned the hard way, how difficult it is to follow when someone is reading from another translation. When I heard bibles closing, I realized a problem.

As the Staff Chaplain at a Regional Medical Hospital, I visited a patient who asked me if we could provide him with an original King James bible during his stay. In all my religious

---

[268] https://www.thegospelcoalition.org/article/how-not-to-argue-about-which-bible-translation-is-best

education I had never heard the original King James version read aloud. So, I hurried back to my office, went to the internet; copied several Psalms and chapter 1 from the book of John. When I gave them to him, he couldn't read any of them and was surprised that the original King James bible was written in old English. I did find a newer KJV version for him to read. Today, there are so many translations that, unless each church selects or chooses a single translation for worship or bible study, few will follow the readings.

There are special translations for women, children and working men, a bible for business men and women, one for new mothers, teenagers, another for bible study or evangelism, and others with the words of Jesus in red letters. **Television evangelists earn thousands if not millions of dollars selling bibles with their name on the cover for their approved version.**[269]

Baptist history, theology and doctrine have undergone significant changes using more modern translations. Baptists disagree on

---

[269] https://www.gci.org/bible/matthew108

theology, but a common study bible has lots of possibilities and benefits. **See the internet article listed below.**[270] All churches are a combination of theologies, depending on the issue. Most Baptists do not care or are theologically indifferent to these differences. To say that Baptist theology is a perfect interpretation of scripture is a misnomer. Baptists' autonomy is too strong for a single theological opinion. For example, is salvation predetermined or not? I have heard salvation preached differently depending on the denomination or the minister's theology.

Paul's view in Romans is that God pre-selected us. **John Calvin (1509-1564)**[271] supports this view. While Dutch Reformed theologian Jacobus Arminius (1560–1609) disagreed, **believing God has granted you free will to choose or reject God's grace.**[272] The question is then, what intention does the

---

270

https://en.wikipedia.org/wiki/History_of_the_Calvinist%E2%80%93Arminian_debate

271 http://www.centervilleroad.com/articles/calvinism-3.html

272

http://www.christianitytoday.com/history/people/theologians/jacob-arminius.html

leader have for choosing one version over another? I cannot answer that question. The church's minister should share his/her research for making that decision.

Some bibles, like the Scofield Bible, have footnotes to help the reader understand these biblical truths as Scofield understood and interpreted them.[273] Different interpretations are not unique to Baptists. Protestants still battle on issues about who's interpretation is right. Church attendance can be either an educational moment for understanding congregational beliefs or a repetition of religious dogma every week.

Which Bible translation *is closest to the original* is an excellent place to begin a discussion. Baptists are often caught in the trap of repeating talking points, heard in Sunday School or from the minister's pulpit. An elderly woman believed I should read from the King James Bible because her previous minister said it was the **only officially authorized version for Protestants.**[274] There

---

[273] John Hagee NKJV, Prophecy Study Bible, Hardcover, Red Letter Edition:

[274] https://www.jesus-is-lord.com/thebible.htm

is no perfect translation of scripture for two simple reasons.

First, no language can be perfectly translated into another language. There are too many idiomatic expressions, cultural values, morals and interpretations of lifestyles that do not fit into another culture. Secondly, we only have copies of the **original scriptures, which contain various and different readings.**[275] Different wordings, inerrancy, accuracy, or wordings don't really matter. **The question is…if I read it, do I believe it, and will I use it to affect my lifestyle?**[276]

For every Christian who reads a bible verse, a decision is made whether to believe it to guide my life. If my children cursed me, scripture tells me how to punish them…**For anyone who curses his father, or his mother shall surely be put to death; he has cursed his father or his mother; his blood is upon**

---

[275] https://www.biblica.com/resources/bible-faqs/is-the-bible-we-have-today-in-english-the-same-as-the-original-bible/

[276] My view on scripture

him.[277]   There is little difference in this Old Testament verse and other ancient writings. The Qur'an says…**Allah does not accept the (duty) and (charitable) prayers of the one who has rebelled against parents.**[278]

The answer is no, I will not put my children to death if they curse me. Am I wrong? No! So, the question is…do I believe these verses, and will I apply them to my life or others? If not, it doesn't matter who says you must believe it or else something terrible will happen to you. The interesting thing is they don't believe all the teaching in the bible either.

Second, it is my belief that there can never be a perfect Bible translation, since we will never know the author's true intent. While the writers may have been inspired, editors and scribes were not. There are too many errors to guarantee a perfect translation. Sometimes we can only guess what the bible authors meant when using some words in a particular sentence. A good Hebrew/Greek Lexicon will give you dozens of different English words that

---

[277] Leviticus 20:9 (RSV)

[278] https://askaquestionto.us/question-answer/family/disobedience-to-parents

may mean the same as the Greek or Hebrew verse or come very close. Choose a difficult passage from your bible. Look it up on the internet using the footnote below for examples of different interpretations.[279]

But then, Baptists scholars will argue over which of these words gives a better meaning for the translation. This tells me that it is their interpretation that makes a difference. Some ministers believe it doesn't matter because the Holy Spirit has breathed approval into the words we have... **All scripture is inspired by God and profitable for teaching, for reproof, for correction and training in righteousness that the man of God may be complete, quipped for every good work**.[280]

That is a pretty big job for every translator when it is an interpretation of a copy. How can this be? Paul's scripture was the Old Testament Law. If Paul's instructions, to Timothy, meant his words in the New Testament were inspired, then some of his letters were inspired before they were written.

---

[279] http://biblehub.com/romans/1-12.htm
[280] 2 Timothy 3:15 (RSV)

And he even admits there are things he doesn't know.[281]

Christians should remember…the New Testament was not finalized until the 3rd century. This was long after all the New Testament writers were dead. Early churches rejected books they felt were not true or worthy of being included…**The Gospel of Thomas, The Epistle of Barnabas, Epistle of Clement, et.al, are examples of books written early in biblical times and used in some, but not all early Christian churches.**[282]

It was years later when man-led councils determined the bible as we have it today. **Then, Martin Luther took out books that were approved for Catholics.**[283] Mormons consider the *Book of Mormon* as a supplement to the King James bible. **Denominations and ministers quote scriptures with different interpretations for heaven, hell, and the**

281

http://www.patheos.com/blogs/crossexamined/2015/09/how-reliable-is-apostle-paul-when-he-knew-very-little-about-jesus/

[282] http://www.bible.ca/b-canon-rejected-books.htm

[283] https://en.wikipedia.org/wiki/Council_of_Trent

final judgements.[284] There as many different interpretations for the book of Revelation as there are authors. How then, does a Christian find a bible that will give them truths to live by? Paul talked about failing to grow up as a Christian…**And I, brethren, could not speak to you as to spiritual men, but as to men of flesh, as to infants in Christ. I gave you milk to drink, not solid food; for you were not yet able to receive it. Indeed, even now you are not yet able, for you are still fleshly. For since there is jealousy and strife among you, are you not fleshly, and are you not walking like mere men? For when one says, I am of Paul, and another, I am of Apollos, are you not mere men?**[285]

Forgive my naiveté, but wouldn't that mean starting with something simple, you can read, and understand? Then, when you are ready, look for a deeper translation for distinctions that may be needed for better application. You do not have to be a scholar to get helpful thoughts

---

[284] https://www.wayoflife.org/database/fireoutofhell.html
[285] 1 Corinthian 3:1-3 (NASB)

and guidance out of an understandable bible translation.

My father used to say...**you get what you pay for and if it is free it's probably not worth much**.[286]Advice truly is cheap, plentiful, and often useless. The internet has a library of questionable options and choices. So does every Baptist church in your community. There are answers from your local radio talk show, newspaper and neighbor's churches that may or may not be reputable. Where you start begins with the question, *what is it you are looking for?* Is Christianity, as practiced in a church or in a religion that is giving you hope and help? Is a bible just somebody's interpretation of words about what is important to gain something only in another life? Or is there a life changing message for today?

The bible is a wonderful book for the history and struggles of Jews and Christians trying to find meaning and purpose for life. In my view, it may only provide part of what you are looking for. Having served as a military chaplain, I

286

https://en.wiktionary.org/wiki/you_get_what_you_pay_for

worked with chaplains, service members and their families that had a variety of religious views and backgrounds. There is some good, and not so good, in all of them. We can learn from each other what is right, good and beneficial for a lifestyle or world view.

Try a ***Huffington Post* article to get you started thinking in the right direction.**[287] Who's right? I cannot say, for I have found comfort and good in what others have taught and told me about their beliefs. Baptists have goodness too, but you have to look for it. Look below the surface at their words and emphasis for the value as it is expressed in those who reflect a quality lifestyle. All great churches provide hope, help, and peace. They may use five different bible translations or allow you to use your own. The final action must always be your own decision…how to apply biblical wisdom to my own life.

It isn't just any bible, nor translation of the bible that makes a difference. How could a

---

[287] https://www.huffingtonpost.com/gleb-tsipursky/searching-for-meaning-and-purpose-in-life-religion-is-optional

different translation of this bible verse from 1 Timothy 2:15, encourage, or give hope to a woman who isn't married or if she or her husband are biologically unable to conceive a child?...**But women will be saved through childbearing--if they continue in faith, love and holiness with propriety.**[288]

I raised this question earlier in this chapter. What are you going to believe and what are you going to practice that makes life meaningful for you and not what is the correct translation for the Hebrew or Greek words. Yoga meets the meditation and physical needs for Christians, and other religious people around the world every day. For some it is religion, others for physical health and for many, both. Yoga may or may not be good for you. The King James bible, under the preaching and teaching of a dedicated caring minister, may answer your search.

Your needs may be found in a large church with all the amenities or a smaller one with a close fellowship. It could be with the television evangelist at home or in a quiet thoughtful

---

[288] 1 Timothy 2:15 - NIV)

setting reading a modern translation. Beware of a television evangelist minister, theologian or anyone who has all the answers. The answer might be simple or complex, depending on what will you do with the interpretations, philosophies, dogma, or guidelines they suggest? The bible can be a tool for your lifestyle discovery or words from someone who uses you for their own benefit.

The phrase...**Know thyself was not invented by Socrates. It is a motto inscribed on the frontispiece of the Temple of Delphi.**[289] Think about it. You are the one who has to do more than hear or read about the need for change. **You can change and adapt ideas into actions and behaviors to benefit you your church, or community.**[290]

Two university women professors, Manns and Rising, have written a couple of books on *Fearless Change*, dealing with how to get a discussion going on any of these topics. They have done the work to get you started. **All you**

---

[289] http://www.the-philosophy.com/socrates-know-yourself
[290] https://www.mindbodygreen.com/-ways-to-get-motivated-start-taking-charge-of-your-life.

have to do is make the commitment and get a conversation started?[291] Life does not have to be the way it is now forever. There are values and exciting ways to live out your Christian life that are still undiscovered. If you choose to take a step of faith, the door is open for a less troublesome lifestyle.

---

[291] More Fearless Change, strategies for making your ideas happen, "Know Yourself" page 81

Chapter 13

WHO TOLD YOU THIS IS THE WAY IT HAS TO BE?

O n the ordering of important things, **people use different procedures and schemes for determining what road to take.**[292] When purchasing new products, like clothing and appliances, they might determine that length of usability more important than price. When purchasing automobiles, the lowest cost may determine which product is selected.

When it comes to denominations and churches, a seeker might use a variety of methodologies, depending on an issue. Is the social gospel or biblical literalism important? Is attendance or membership going to affect, generally or specifically, my family, or friends? In a survey, 50% said family, friends and

---

[292] https://link.springer.com/chapter/10.1007/978-3-319-13105-4_56

opportunities for **special types of ministries drew them to a particular congregation.**[293]

Another survey revealed that 58% selected a church for its doctrinal or theological interpretation they agreed with.[294] In another survey, the church's location was a 70% factor and these percentage were up over surveys taken ten years earlier. Cultural practices must also be factored in with personal and religious reasoning.

Tribalism is always an option, according to one writer's definition...**you don't actually have to think very much. All you need to know on any given subject is which side you're on. You pick up signals from everyone around you, you slowly winnow your acquaintances to those who will reinforce your worldview, a tribal leader**

---

[293] https://churchrelevance.com/qa-top-reasons-for-church-attendance/

[294] https://www.evangelismcoach.org/top-reasons-unchurched-people-choose-a-church/

calls the shots, and everything slips into place.[295]

The sought-after conclusion usually will determine which methodology is used. Does a doctrine, preaching style, music, location, or fellowship influence the decision to become a Baptist, Methodist, Catholic, Mormon or Adventist? Yes, it does, as survey data continue to show. Religious data are seldom static. Changes occur with every new survey as demographics and churches, change. My point is, what Christianity is today, is not what it was twenty or a thirty years ago, and it will not be ten years from now, what it is today.

It might be that ministers and doctoral public education students have something in common. Both believe that to get promoted, they must move up the ladder into larger organizations for success. **For both, a new mega building on a huge campus, seems like the best way to get there.**[296] Success should be measured on better people and

[295] Andrew Sullivan in New Yorker magazine, quoted in The Week 10/6/2017. page 12

[296] https://irrco.wordpress.com/2010/06/10/how-to-start-a-mega-church-in-7-steps/

communities rather than new buildings or the number of programs completed.

When the minister's sermon topic is on immigration or politics, the listener should select which strategy or process they will use to accept, adapt, or reject the message. Some of the differences that affect the response depend on whether the member is active, inactive, or just an attendee. Labels like conservative or liberal, as well as differing beliefs about race, and cultural morals and values may be factored into any discussion on immigration. I found it was easy to get a congregation's money for missions and harder to discuss or sponsor refugees over here.

Missions over there, not *immigration here* finds more support in most Christian churches. Tribalism is alive and well in Christian churches. Comfort sets in when change is not suggested. Most sermons do not get more than 30-40% agreement, when applied personally. It may be a surprise to some that most of those who are in agreement with sermons, believe it, because it applies to someone else, somewhere else and not to themselves.

If a church or culture holds a very conservative public or private view on sin, or sexual matters, then you might choose a church whose ministry supports Paul's warning...**do you not know that the unrighteous will not inherit the kingdom of God? Do not be deceived; neither immoral, nor idolaters, nor adulterers, nor homosexuals, nor thieves, nor the greedy, nor drunkards, nor revilers, nor robbers, will inherit the kingdom of God.**[297]

Women might feel that there should be more rigid dress codes for schoolgirls. Males, with a conservative outlook, might extend the rules beyond girls to women showing cleavage, blue or purple hair color, eye shadow, lip gloss, tattoos, or nose, lip, and facial jewelry. For centuries there have been religious codes for diversity in dress codes that became cultural. We are familiar with cloistered habits for nuns, monks, and priests. Jewish hair styles, beards, hats, and other dress identify their fundamentalism. Dress simplicity that avoids gaudy dresses, distinguishes the Amish and

---

[297] 1 Corinthians 6:9-10 (RSV)

Mennonite religious cultures. A hundred years ago, Christian ministers' facial hair was in, then off again or changing to longer sideburns. The long black dress coat was popular for clergy in many Baptist churches.

Are these issues the ones that really need to be discussed in our churches today? Here is another example...a *Missouri church dismissed their pastor because he did not use the Billy Graham style for holding up his bible when speaking from the pulpit.* These things are hidden behind the cultural values that determine membership, worship styles, as well as morals and values. It doesn't have to be this way. Church is about building character, changing lives and communities, not a congregation that looks or acts alike.

If these issues affect me personally, then I have a stronger interest in getting involved. Selecting a church and getting involved in a church's ministry is more complicated than churches want to believe. Time is more than money. It has value for who you are and what you choose to do with your most important resource...life.

Americans, love their autonomy and political freedom. Most do not want to be told what to do, who to support, vote for, or against. Baptists do not want to be told what they must believe, accept or adhere to in secular values or morals. But, that doesn't mean people shouldn't accept different viewpoints. This double standard is a common practice among Christians today. The United States Constitution, Article VI states...**Senators and Representatives before mentioned, and the members of the several State Legislatures, and all executive and judicial officers, both of the United States and of the several States, shall be bound by Oath or Affirmation, to support this Constitution; but no religious test shall ever be required as a qualification to any office or public trust under the United States.**[298] That is the law!

But that doesn't mean when a person goes into the voting booth and has a prejudice for or against a particular religious group, that they will or will not vote against an otherwise

---

[298]https://www.usconstitution.net/xconst_A6.html

qualified candidate. Some Baptists, willingly accepted John Kennedy Catholicism and rejected Mitt Romney's Mormonism as a cult. Atheism and religion is still a test for some voters who believe and quote the constitution.

It really isn't strange that Baptists practice a double standard. They have one standard for themselves and another for the other person's failures, sins, and short-sighted views. I know Baptist ministers who smoke, drink alcohol, have been guilty of lusting after women, told dirty jokes, used profanity, and embezzled money, and broke local, state, and federal laws.

I know Baptist farmers who do not smoke but, raise tobacco and do not drink yet sell corn and other grains for alcoholic beverages. I have counseled Baptist men and women who knew they were violating the teachings of their church, when tempted, but did it anyway. So, nobody is perfect...including me. Why then do we have so many rules and laws that Baptists don't intend to keep? It is interesting that we expect others to abide by these laws, rules and guidelines, but we can occasionally or intentionally break them. Why, as ministers, do we preach so often on sins of the flesh? I followed a minister who preached on adultery once or twice a month until his wife figured out the subject was his problem, confronted him and ended their marriage and his ministry. My guess is that what topics ministers preach about is because they think it is what the members want them to speak about. Remember when I preached tobacco was sinful, and Brother Harry reminded me it was his only real cash crop and if he didn't raise tobacco, he couldn't give money to the church. Good point Harry! Should I be his minister for free? Don't ask! You see, we all have our vested interests.

For most of my sixty years in ministry, my classes in religion, philosophy, psychology, and sociology couldn't convince me that education alone could get anyone to do what they really didn't want to do. I unsuccessfully tried taking away privileges, public exposure, denial of financial support, anger, shouting, pouting, abstinence, and even suggested divorce. I believe now you can't guarantee happiness, participation, or support by legislating laws and rules.

Americans, Christians, and Baptists feel free to do what they want to do, whether there is a law or rule for or against it. Financial ruin, prison, public shame, and/or divorce won't stop them. Since none of this works, why do we keep pushing the idea that if we shout louder or talk long enough, we can get people to believe like we want them to believe? Religious Liberty is foundational for Baptists. **Baptists are almost unanimous in rejecting the Puritan's attitude toward Roger Williams that led to his removal from Massachusetts.**[299]

Before the Puritans kicked Williams out of Massachusetts, he founded the First Baptist Church in American circa 1638. He tried hard to show his Puritan brothers a better way, but they were not listening. **His influence did have some influence on the Bill of Rights, freedom of conscience and the separation of church and state.**[300] However, he had little influence on Puritans. Baptists support Roger Williams' struggles for separation of church

---

[299] https://www.gotquestions.org/Baptists.html

[300] separation.us/the-origins-of-wall-of-separation/

and state and religious freedom until it applies to something they don't like in a community, and then they want a law to stop it. They want a Christian nation with laws and rules that exclude people with differences. Roger Williams supported the idea that differences were okay.

Let me begin by saying... *this example I am about to give isn't a perfect solution for every Baptist or problem.* However, I do throw this into the mix for consideration. It is not as complicated or as deep as it the title sounds. I was trained and use William Glasser's, "Reality Therapy." He worked for years in California with high school girls in reform schools. In a rigid state system of rules, he developed a process, for helping young women with behavioral problems. It was uncomplicated and simple. **It was a plan that avoids pain and leads the person to accept responsibility for their own behavior.**[301]

Training in Reality Therapy offered me the option to provide a methodology for helping others discover their own path for success and

---

[301] ttps://en.wikipedia.org/wiki/William_Glasser

happiness in a rigid culture or a highly complicated world. If you can't change the culture, then you must change yourself. When you change, others watching you will evaluate you differently and if your way is positive, they'll even try your way for themselves. When your behavior influences others, then your lifestyle may catch on. We do not have to march in goose-step uniformity to show honest and productive morals or values. We do however have to eliminate the double standard for ourselves.

Our differences mostly matter just to us anyway, but some are watching us to see if we really believe what we say. Remember what a young college student stated...**Jesus Christ I can accept. It's Christians I cannot stand.**[302] Who we are and how we accept responsibility for our behavior matters. I cannot be responsible for you, but I can be responsible for myself. We can be different, as long as it doesn't lead to anarchy. In any city with enough Baptist Churches, there will be similarity and

---

[302] A college student at the Billy Graham Crusade, Knoxville, TN May 28, 1970

differences. Wouldn't it be wonderful if we could accept our similarities and with love tolerate our differences?

As a Baptist, I have found a more excellent way that is right for me and I try hard to accept responsibility for all of it. I do not judge others' sexual orientation or beliefs about gender by my own values and morality. All must accept responsibility for themselves within current laws, values, and morals in the culture in which they live.

Of course, there will be criticisms and/or acceptance or rejection depending on each situation. It is true, some employers won't accept our differences. Laws might make this easier or harder. You still must accept responsibility and convince yourself that your actions are yours alone, then you must give other their right to be different. A Christian university denied me the opportunity to teach in their program because I am divorced. I liked teaching for them in the program. But, I understand and accepted their view as right for them and so, then it must be right and okay for me too.

The wonderful thing about religion in our country is that you don't have to belong. You can pick and choose morals and values that are right for you. If you make a mistake, you can change, even if the choices you made were disastrous. It doesn't have to be what someone else says is right, or the only way. You do not have to believe in heaven, hell or the second coming of Jesus in a certain manner or timeline. You can seek and read a variety of resources to help you along the way.

Times change, and our laws change, as our culture changes. Tomorrow's morals and values will not always be as they are now. We all learn to cope with life's problems in one way or another. Advice is plentiful, but the final choices are up to you. individuals may reject you. But, rejection is their problem, not necessarily yours, unless you want to make it so. The **A** for Adventist, the **B** for Baptist, or the **C** for Catholic may or may not fit your needs. We do have choices, and that brings you faith and answers life's questions. Go for it! Whoever told you it has to be their way is, in my opinion wrong.

Chapter 14

CAN BAPTISTS STOP
CULTURE WARS?

I s there an answer to this question? No, there is no simple answer. Research shows...**Baptists are slow to change and, when they do, they go kicking and screaming.**[303] This feeling that they got it right did not die when Martin Luther and Protestants separated from Catholic dogma. For centuries, denominations, church leaders and laity pushed the idea that separating yourself from the world by holding on to what is a set of unchanging values and morals was enough to keep themselves pure. Did their view work? No, it didn't then, and hasn't yet. It took almost a hundred years to prove their Baptist doctrine wasn't going to happen.

Now they have pretty much rejected a view that tried to establish purity outside Protestantism. J. M. Carroll, in a book titled <u>A</u>

---

[303] https://thinkprogress.org/southern-baptist-conference-struggling-lgbt-people-can-change-through

Trail of Blood, tried to show a unbroken line of succession from **Baptists today back to John the Baptist, to prove they were not Protestants.**[304]It was rudely nicknamed, the Jerusalem, Jordon, John theory. Jesus authorized John to baptize him, so John became the first pastor of the **First Baptist congregation in Jerusalem.**[305] Why is pure lineage back to Jesus more important than living a Christian life today? I don't know why. It was then but making the church pure seems to be a driving standard for Baptists today.

There is an old popular Baptist hymn titled, **I Shall Not Be Moved**[306] and it is sung with gusto as foundational for Baptists when the world wants them to change. Church purity for membership and separation from the world is still found in Baptist life. **When Baptist churches believe that you have to be like**

[304] http://stevensperay.wordpress.com/the-history-of-the-Baptist-churches-in-a-nutshell/
[305] Professor, Dr. Wayne Ward, Southern Seminary 1957
[306] Billy Graham School of Evangelism - https://www.hymnlyrics.org/newlyrics_i/i_shall_not_be_moved.php

them to attend or to be a Baptist,[307] **then those on the outside have decided they are not interested.**[308] In my estimation, 85-90% of the culture wars start when religious conservatives want their scriptural authority and denominational purity and dogma placed into public law.

Let's face the fact, that rigid unchanging denominational dogma has put some Baptists in the box with other closed communities like the Amish, Mennonites, and Hutterites. Some are now suggesting that Baptists should withdraw from the world; similar to the idea called _The Benedict_ option...**to form a separate community of prayer and worship. Benedict of Nursia founded monasteries and a well-known "Rule" to govern Christian life together.**[309]

Baptists are already supporting private schools, colleges and universities to keep the

---

[307] http://www.providencecharleston.org/reboot-sermon-series/

[308] www.gotquestions.org/Baptists.html

[309] https://www.washingtonpost.com/news/acts-of-faith/wp/2017/03/02/christians-have-lost-the-culture-wars-should-they-withdraw-from-the-mainstream/?utm_term=.1d79364c8182

world out of influencing students with unacceptable cultural values. It is their right to do so, but they must take responsibility for segregating education from the world and the culture where life and work will be practiced. Humans will always be in need of help and hope. Why then do we reject those who are like us?

A favorite chant among Baptists in the South, for which there is no supporting data, is that the *government has taken the Bible and prayer out of public schools leading to more crime and deviancy.* **Baptists generally are looking for sin outside their church, particularly in public education, where students are asked to think outside the box, accept change, or do their own thinking.**[310]

Unable to change the Supreme Court's decision on public schools, conservative religious groups want to separate from the world with their own schools to keep students from being exposed to cultural values and activities they determine as sinful. So, they

---

[310] https://www.desiringgod.org/messages/the-challenge-of-relativism

preach against anything that tries to take away their traditions or dogma.

This old idea, expressed on a religious website states…be sure or your sins will find you out.[311] How can a church or religious school be pure when the people who run it are imperfect? Baylor University, at this writing, has not solved its latest sports scandal. A Baptist school in my city let the minister and a couple of the school's staff members go when their private sexual affaires became public. Baptist politicians are facing charges of sexual deviancy. Separation from the world will not and cannot guarantee purity.

One of my preaching professors said…**an average Baptist sermon goes like this: members should read the bible more, prayer more, and go out and win more of the lost to Christ.**[312] This is not a bad statement unless this is the only message church members hear. In some cases, it is especially true when the favorite topic is evangelism.

---

[311] https://billmuehlenberg.com/
[312] Authors preaching class 1956

There are no statistics on how many Baptists ministers or members are convinced evangelism is the church's only mission.[313] Hyper-evangelism from a pulpit can give Baptists a problem when the members start knocking on doors and stopping people on the street. If the sermon's methodology was correct, why are so many Baptist churches declining in attendance and have members changing denominations?

Few Christians today are valued because they believe and practice rigid separatist ideals and evangelistic dogma. Finger pointing at sinners in a culture war doesn't seem to be working either. If the culture looks at Baptists and sees something they admired in faith or behavior, then they might come in for a look.

Training more lay members with the *Roman Road* or *The Four Spiritual Laws* has not solved the needs for Baptist churches or their communities. Having taught growth techniques and evangelistic methods, I found these programs do not support church members'

---

[313] The Tennessean 11/4/17 - Could the church save the world? page 19A

spiritual growth. Not every Baptist church needs to be like a Billy Graham crusade or annual revival meeting. If religion is only interested in numbers and not personal growth, continual decline is assured.

Maybe, the answer is not in big new buildings and mega churches, but in rescue missions, soup kitchens, women's shelters, divorce counseling, job counseling, English as a second language, and reaching out to the needs of the stranger in every community. Helping people change is a great way to build better communities.

As a chaplain, my work was never about making chaplains important. It was all about the mission to care for soldiers and their families. Soul winning was never high on the list of things for us to do. Listening, caring, helping people deal with problems and working for our troops' success was what we did best.

Some faith group chaplains didn't see this as their purpose for ministry and they left the army unfilled. I worked with one new faith group chaplain who didn't stay on active duty long because he spent his time trying to **convert soldiers to his faith instead of taking care of**

business.[314] A few ministers have bad-mouthed the social gospel that takes the message of Jesus to people with caring ministry rather than pulpit evangelism.

The social gospel was an early 20th century movement aimed at merging Christianity with social problems. Walter Rauschenbusch was a Northern Baptist and one of the early promoters for social justice using the social gospel. He led a pastoral movement involving churches and laity. The social gospel was often considered liberal theology and more a part of Methodist doctrine than Baptist.

It was Rauschenbush's goal to attack poverty and the systems that promoted it. **Rauschenbusch's work influenced, among others, Martin Luther King; Desmond Tutu; and his grandson, Richard Rorty. Even in the 21st century Rauschenbusch's name is used by certain social-justice ministries in tribute to his life and work, including such groups as the Rauschenbusch Metro Ministries in New York and the**

---

[314] Author's ministry at U.S. Army Chaplain Center and School 1992-93

Rauschenbusch Center for Spirit and Action in Seattle.[315]

Can Baptists on the left and right work together on social ministries? There certainly is scriptural support for it...**Whatever you did for one of my brothers or sisters, no matter how unimportant they seemed, you did for me.**[316] It's true that Baptist ministries come in many sizes, styles and flavors.

Our African American congregations spend time and effort getting voters to the polls to elect social justice leaders who will **remove restrictions that segregate or restrict people of color**.[317]

Latino Baptists focus on helping integrate immigrant families with support and information on **how live on their community**.[318] White Baptist congregations seem more interested in replicating congregations that look like themselves.

---

[315] https://en.wikipedia.org/wiki/Walter_Rauschenbusch
[316] Matthew 25:40 (GWT)
[317] http://www.nydailynews.com/news/politics/black-churches-move-souls-polls-latino-voters
[318] https://www.wgm.org/hispanicusa-church

Conservative and fundamental Baptists have their opinions and solutions, which tend to be separatist and dissenting rather than cooperating. Sometimes, there are more opinions in a congregation, than there are people actually working together doing ministry.

If you selected a methodology for social justice implementation, it might be possible to take a two-pronged approach for cooperation. One approach deals with the causes for economic poverty, such as slum housing, Jim Crow laws, civil rights abuses, and laws which affect building a community's reputation and effectiveness.

A second approach focuses on helping individuals whom the culture has abandoned. These include the poor, the homeless, and those in need of food, job training, clothing and shelter. These ministries are not limited to the inner cities. Baptists need to be more heavily involved in changing laws to protect women, children and the homeless, from abuse, slavery, and crime. The speed with which American culture is changing opens the door for ministries to address an endless stream of changing economic, and social values. There is plenty of work to be done in many of these fields and both approaches toward finding solutions have their supporters. When congress and states passed similar versions of the Religious Freedom Restoration Act in the 1990's, **the laws required that there be compelling interest to restrict a person's free exercise of religion.**[319] These laws only muddied the waters as Christians and Baptists took different roads to try and solve social problems.

Some court clerks refused to sign marriage licenses for gays, sighting religious convictions.[320] The split between the Southern Baptists and Cooperative Baptists was heightened when the issue came to gay marriage. **The Southern Baptists said they were unprejudiced;**[321] yet took a rigid

---

319

https://en.wikipedia.org/wiki/Religious_Freedom_Restoration_Act

[320] http://www.npr.org/sections/thetwo-way/gay-couples-lawsuit-against-kentucky-clerk

[321] https://www.southern-baptist-convention-claims-harbor-no-ill-will-toward-lgbt-people-it

rejection of churches that disagreed. **One example is Cooperative Baptist churches who took a more liberal view, supporting individuals' right to marry and remain church members.**[322] Baptists may not win the culture war, but they can help stop human suffering by working with groups and organizations that care for human needs.

Adults have at least one thing in common with all faith groups, and that is, if they disagree enough with doctrine or church dogma, they respond with their feet and totally leave or move to another faith group. **Those who leave, have their reasons, and the biggest one is, no-one can require that they stay.**[323]

---

[322] https://Baptistnews.com/article/Baptist-church-votes-to-ok-gay-marriage/
[323] https://baptistnews.com/article/as-millennials-leave-the-church-

Chapter 15

YES, THERE IS A SOLUTION TO THE BAPTIST PROBLEM!

W hat does it mean to claim the name Baptist? I believe I have presented my case, that Baptists do not and never will agree on theology, doctrine, polity, and administration. Dissent may not be something that is universally granted. However, for Baptists, dissent is a right, accepted and practiced. This is true from the highest denominational level and down to the local churches and members. No one size fits all, never has been for Baptists, and probably never will. But descent will stay in discussions.

Any group, church or person can claim the name Baptist for themselves, without fear of violating copyright laws or legal reprisals. Likewise, Baptists are strong on religious liberty and the right to be free from governmental control and influence. Religious liberty is as old as Roger Williams' dissent in Massachusetts, before our nation was founded. Of course, opinions, disagreements, discussions, and different viewpoints about who is right and who is wrong will continue. But that goes on now, anyway. So where should Baptists go from here? Is there a solution that might be beneficial to all? Yes, there is a solution, but not everyone will be pleased.

Baptists already own and practice the solution, they just don't want to admit it. As I have mentioned, Baptists love independence and believe in a narrow religious liberty definition for themselves. Baptist churches can practice closed communion, baptism by means other than immersion, membership without forgiveness, pot-luck suppers, Santa Claus, and Easter eggs hunts in the church worship center. The real issues are who is offended by all this contested discourse and how serious are these issues and differences?

One unsuccessful solution has been for the denomination to kick out a dissenting church from belonging because of a doctrinal or polity issue. Another unsuccessful solution is for a church, knowing it will be ostracized, choosing to remove itself from the larger body. There are thousands of Baptist churches and groups already choosing to align themselves in new and different subgroups. Isn't this what independence means? Baptists are fully capable of self-government without a hierarchy telling them what is right. Today, more are not agreeing with a hierarchical leadership where men mainly set the rules for what it takes to belong to the larger body. What would happen if Baptists took the lead and agreed that it is okay to be different in theology, doctrine, and polity? Each then, with their own standards, goals, and objectives, could work together, where they can, on projects and purposes they agree on, and love those others who choose not to cooperate and/or participate with them.

Atheists, agnostics, and unbelievers would see that religion means acceptance not separation or discrimination. Immigrants, men and women of color and mixed races could be called Baptist. Homosexuals, gays, lesbians, and transgenders could be members of Baptist churches. Ex-felons, prostitutes, pedophiles, and drug addicts could worship together and seek God's will in a loving, giving and supporting Baptist Church. The rich and poor, working together, might find common ground to share worship space and support. **Please**

don't be overcome by this suggestion. It is already happening,[324] not on a large scale, but one at a time. **Baptists are breaking the mold that says you must be like *this* to belong**[325] Work together on what is important for each church, tolerate differences, to build successful churches and communities. Unity, when it is possible and toleration, when differences exist, is achievable.

Faultfinding is unproductive. If you do not agree with denominational rules, go on your own way and demonstrate Christian values and morals and lifestyles in your community. There is no one church standard for Baptists. We don't have to belong to a group to do God's work. In some cases, we can do it better alone without dictation from above.

If Baptists can make it work in some places, why not let the likes come together instead of insisting on universal unanimity and purity to claim the name Baptist? Why not admit that is already happening, within all Baptist

---

324

http://www.assaultweb.net/forums/showthread.php?t=27569

[325] http://www.firstbelleglade.com/who/

congregations where there are silent differences? In some churches members are choosing not to make their differences an issue.

Here is a second idea. Most church buildings are not fully used. Why can't more than one Baptist church or social group use the same building? This also is happening with Korean, Mung, and Hispanic congregations that meet at different times. There are churches that support women's ministry and homeless shelters, English as a second language, Alcohol Anonymous, and clothing and food distribution centers.

Recently a group of Baptists in Nashville joined with other faith groups speaking out against white supremacy meetings.[326] What if Baptist groups started supporting different social gospel issues, cultural problems and wanted to share facilities and costs rather than doctrinal positions? I know of a Methodist church that has ministries for the poor, drug addicts, a women's shelter and grief counseling as well as all the amenities for a

[326] The Nashville Tennessean October 10, 2017, page 3A

large active First United Methodist church. They provide the money and staff for ministries where the needs are found without pushing for membership to get the bragging rights. It says something that we care and will help even if you choose not to belong.

What keeps these ideas from happening is the Baptist idea that a church congregation should be pure, segregated, and separated from the world by theology, doctrine and polity. Many feel that churches should be located in a fine large building with lots of nice facilities, parking, and staff to meet the particular needs of a few, like themselves. Its ministries should focus on evangelism and missions overseas or in some other community since there are some who may not be acceptable for this church.

As a chaplain working with service members who had a variety of problems, I found belonging to a church would not solve many military problems. There were few soldiers who wanted to become a Baptist to solve their problem. Baptism wasn't the answer either. As a Baptist chaplain I didn't have to ask a soldier to be a Christian to help him or her and solve their problem. I could be a resource and enter into a discussion that often fell outside of my theology and doctrine. What would happen if Baptists looked beyond demanding unity and started meeting human needs?

I know a married couple who accepted everyone for who they were at that moment. One had grown up Baptist the other Jewish. They were always willing to listen or discuss something of interest to you. Leonard and Gerri never criticized you for your comments or opinions. **They listened and interacted only when they felt they had something to contribute rather than refute.**[327]

Every community needs hundreds like them. Would communities respect ministries more if they were unbiased to people of color, gender, and ideology? What if, in solving community problems, religious groups were seen in light of their love, support and care? Look at your church and its ministry and start a discussion about the best road for your church to do ministry in your community.

---

[327] The Tennessean - Americans must listen to understand... 10/29/17, page 13A

At eighty years of age, I am teaching a class in a retirement community on Religion and Culture to help discuss our religious differences and work together to affect our community's communication and cooperation. Hopefully, then we have a chance to work together on projects that will build us up instead of taking down our friends and neighbors.

ABOUT THE AUTHOR

Jim Rennell has enjoyed successful careers as a military officer, Baptist minister, and educator. He was endorsed by the American, Southern and Cooperative Baptist Denominations. Having served as a Chaplain and minister and denominational representative in all three, his experience with pastors, educators, and denominational workers gives him an extensive background into the life and practice of Baptists.

He has recently taken up writing articles and publishing books as a hobby. He has published two books on humor and one Bible study, with the hopes that he can bring some joy and happiness to his readers.

In his military career he rose from a paratrooper Private to Sergeant. Ten years later, after completing formal education, he returned to the military as a chaplain. He spent twenty-seven years, starting out as a First Lieutenant and retiring as a Bird Colonel.

After his military career, he taught as an adjunct professor, teaching courses in history, interpersonal relations and adult education.

Evaluating his career moves, he said it looks like he couldn't hold a job for long.

Jim's three previous books are available on Amazon.com: **Senior Humor, Humor in the Church**, and **The Power of Words**.

Order Copies From
Ch (Col) Jim Rennell
459 E. Stevens St.
Cookeville, TN 38501
(931) 265-2248
Chap502@charter.net